STALIN

MAN OF STEEL OR MASS MURDERER?

MICHAEL KERRIGAN

amber
BOOKS

Published by
Amber Books Ltd
United House
North Road
London
N7 9DP
United Kingdom
www.amberbooks.co.uk
Appstore: itunes.com/apps/amberbooksltd
Facebook: www.facebook.com/amberbooks
Twitter: @amberbooks

ISBN: 978-1-78274-741-3

Project Editor: Michael Spilling
Designer: Hart McLeod Ltd
Picture Research: Terry Forshaw

Printed in Italy

1 4 6 8 10 9 7 5 3 2

Contents

INTRODUCTION

Ruthlessly effective...? Or just ruthless? His country's saviour or its enslaver and near-destroyer? Few lives have been quite as contentious as that of Joseph Stalin.

Neighbours were well accustomed to the sound of small-arms fire from the Butovo estate. This sometime stud farm just south of Moscow had for several years been a training school for the NKVD. The 'People's Commissariat for Internal Affairs' were the Soviet Union's not-so-secret secret police.

Opposite: Authority and strength personified: Stalin as he was seen in 1952 by his loyal subject the Estonian painter Johannes Saal (1911–64).

Naturally, they had their own firing range.

In the latter part of 1937, however, activities on the estate intensified. The rate of rifle fire rattled up a gear or two. Locals noticed trucks and cars coming and going at every hour of the day and night. Clamorous fusillades rang out, to be followed by lengthy silences while who knew what went on. (Pretty soon, of course, they had begun to guess...) It's a matter of record now that over 20,000 supposed enemies of the Soviet state were killed here in the course of the 'Great Purge' – sometimes several hundred in a single day.

Their bodies, buckling before the firing squads, were thrown together into mass graves before being quickly covered over and forgotten.

MOTLEY MARTYRS

Decades later, after the fall of Communism, researchers began working through the old state archives, building up a picture of those who had ended up beneath the soil of what was now being consecrated as a shrine. Many who had fallen here had been Orthodox priests, and by the early years of the twenty-first century the Church was making a memorial for them here.

Interred alongside these slaughtered priests were scores and hundreds of laymen and laywomen – and, indeed, a great many Marxist martyrs. Although they'd rejected the teachings of the Church, they were by any normal definition decent people. If they had rejected religion, they certainly hadn't discarded its imperative of doing good: rather than trust to eternity, though, they had hoped to improve Russia in the here and now. Committed Communists, they had nevertheless fallen foul of the unforgiving authorities in their Party for whom the slightest deviation from the line they had ordained represented treason.

Others hadn't been saintly by any standards: some were Communist officials who had enthusiastically persecuted others for their supposed ideological shortcomings before being denounced for 'deviancy' in their turn in the paranoid political merry-go-round of the time. Still others had been no more than common criminals. Given the existence of the Soviet state in a semi-permanent state of emergency, though, the most banal and trivial offences could be seen as attempted subversions of the official order.

Right: Religious services are held at the old Butovo firing range in memory of the thousands massacred by Stalin's henchmen.

BREAD OF DEATH

Take the case of Misha Shamonin, an orphan only thirteen years old: his conviction was for stealing two loaves of bread. In the mugshot taken after his arrest, we see him almost drowning in the folds of a greatcoat that's far too big for him: even so, his expression is stoical, resigned. Young as he was, he had lived long enough to acquire the weary fatalism common to his older contemporaries; the certainty that the state simply would not be opposed. And so it proved: on 7 December 1937, Misha met his death. In recognition of his tender years, he was spared the firing squad: a single gunshot to the back of his head sufficed. His documentation was crudely altered, to bring his age up to fifteen (the minimum mandated then for legal execution), then his body was thrown into a pit with dozens more.

Communism's founder, Karl Marx (1818–83), in *Capital* (1867) had inveighed against the fate of those 'ragged, half-starved, untaught children' given up to work in industry by their desperate parents. The whole point of the workers' state was that its people should be supported by the society they themselves supported with their labours. ('From each according to his ability, to each according to his needs.') Its families should escape such suffering; their children be spared so bleak a destiny. An urchin out of a Dickens novel – hungry, poor and unprotected; a child whose home was the city's streets – Misha had no business even existing in the Soviet Union.

MARXIST MORALITY

Now, of course, thanks to the agents of the NKVD, he didn't. The rightful order had been restored: the system worked – as a sado-bureaucracy, at least. As scathing as it had always been about the injustices attendant upon the market economy, Communism had never claimed to be about

Below: In his memorial mugshot, Misha Shamonin shows the stoicism of so many millions who suffered injustice in the Stalin era.

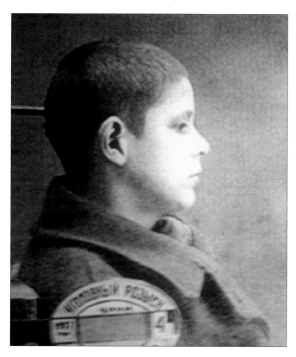
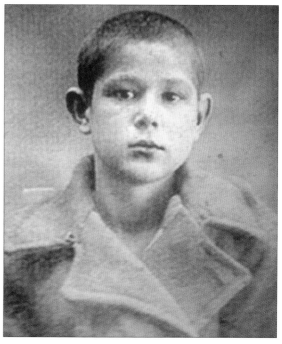

kindness or compassion. Marx had despised these 'bourgeois' virtues as the sops thrown to the oppressed by their oppressors – and the conscience-salving comfort the oppressors administered to themselves.

By the same token, he had no time for what he called 'utopian' idealism: there was nothing to be gained by yearning and hoping for a better world. You can see his point – even if it's harder, perhaps, to understand his conviction that the better society would build itself through the inevitable workings of economics and of history. Communism, he argued, roughly, would come about of its own accord as capitalism came apart under the stresses and strains of its inherent 'contradictions'.

LENIN TAKES THE LEAD

Russia's rulers since 1917 had maintained that this radical reconstruction was under way – with a little help and encouragement from them. Acknowledging their departure from Marxist orthodoxy, they characterized their philosophy as 'Marxism-Leninism'. Lenin had pretty much created Soviet Communism in his own image: his key contribution, however, had been his insistence that Marxism's historical 'grand narrative' could be, as it were, edited – its slow but inexorable evolution towards socialism helped along by the intervention of a small

but resolute 'vanguard' of revolutionaries. Marx himself, had his posthumous advice been sought, would almost certainly have told Lenin to come back in another century's time when Russia had a modern economy worth the name. In Marx's carefully-delineated scheme of things, the revolution could only be the work of a skilled and sophisticated industrial 'proletariat' of the type to be found in Britain and Germany.

Above: What, we can wonder, would the old man have made of his legacy? The founder of modern Communism, Karl Marx (1818–83).

In Russia, by contrast, such a class could barely be said to exist: the mass of the people lived in agrarian poverty, backward and illiterate, in thrall to their landowners and priests. Lenin was entitled to feel, though, that in a country clearly crying out for change, he could be forgiven for cutting a few corners here and there.

Books by the thousand were subsequently to be written by scholars in the Soviet Union and elsewhere exploring and unpacking all the different implications of Lenin's big idea.

One thing is certain, though: if Marxism-Leninism brought forward the attainment of some kind of Communism from what had been a vague and indefinite future into a historic present, it gave the Party enormous authority – and its leader potentially awe-inspiring power.

Below: They're smiling here, long-suffering as they are, but by 1900 Russia's peasants certainly needed some sort of revolutionary change.

IRON DISCIPLINE

Russia's Social Democrats – Marxist revolutionaries – had at the conclusion of their Second Party Congress in London in 1903 divided into two factions: the *mensheviks* ('those of the minority'), led by Juliy Martov (1873–1923) had wanted a loose and open party structure in which individuals would be able to speak their minds. Vladimir Ilyich Ulyanov (1870–1924), better known now by his codename *Lenin* ('Man of Iron'), had led the majority *bolshevik* faction with his call for the Party to be a tightly-knit group of strictly disciplined revolutionaries.

Lenin's *nom de guerre* was eminently appropriate: he was tough and unyielding – understandably, given the sacrifices he'd had to make to his Marxist cause. The *Okhrana*, the Czarist secret police, had executed his elder brother Aleksandr (1866–87) for his part in an attempt

> ## Democracy was too important to be left to the capricious decisions of individual electors.

to assassinate Czar Alexander III (1845–94). His sisters Anna Ulyanovna (1864–1935) and Maria Ilyinichna Ulyanovna (1878–1937) were also involved in the Social Democratic struggle,

Above: Impassioned as always, Lenin addresses the 1903 Party Congress.

as was his younger brother Dmitri Ilyich (1874–1943). The revolution had become his life, long before the events of 1917: by that time he'd had to spend several decades on the run.

The experience had left him with both an implacable hatred for the Czarist authorities and an adamantine belief in what determination and discipline could achieve. Democracy was too important to be left to chance, and to the capricious decisions of individual electors: the Party should wield power on the People's behalf.

Communism was a liberating force, its leaders claimed. But liberation has to have its limits, they pointed out. For civilized life to be possible, there has to be some compromise between the desires of the individual and the greater good; freedom cannot be completely limitless. And it's true: to some extent, every advanced democracy restricts its people's rights and effectively curtails their liberties with its laws. Russia's Bolshevik rulers believed that for the class which had exploited and oppressed the people to be allowed the chance of claiming back their privileges was the opposite of democracy.

Not only should this class be denied a voice: it should be comprehensively suppressed. 'War to the death against the rich and their hangers-on, the bourgeois intellectuals ...' wrote Lenin. Even allowing for rhetorical excess, it's clear that he based his moral authority and that of his Soviet government on the energy and unswerving zeal with which it set out to put down the country's elites – on the land, in industry and commerce.

RULING ASSUMPTIONS

Long before Lenin's death in 1924, then, the template was well established for a certain kind of rule. If the Party's power was to be absolute, the authority of its leader within it was to be all but unchallenged. The power of the 'working class' was actually to be wielded by one man.

Along with this went, if not an avowed policy, then at least a deeply ingrained habit of rallying support for what might otherwise be unwelcome and unpopular programmes by denouncing and attacking internal enemies. (And, of course, external ones, though in this respect the Soviet state was really no different from any other populist government of this or any other time. Given

Above: British troops in Murmansk, 1918. Western intervention after the revolution only heightened the paranoia the Bolsheviks already felt.

the invasions of Russia mounted by powers like Britain and France in the revolution's immediate aftermath, suspicion of the capitalist West made perfect sense.)

And great things were indeed achieved by Stalin's Soviet Union – albeit at such appalling cost that the gains seemed dubious at best. Stalin did, however, see his country through three decades, an epic programme of industrialization and agrarian reform and a World War – even if he left behind an exhausted and traumatized Russian people.

EMBLEMATIC IMAGE

These points have to be made – it may seem, laboured – because, when we talk about Stalin and his life, we're almost invariably talking about other things as well. Any biography has to address the discontinuity between its subject's private person and public 'persona'. With a subject so notorious as Stalin, that challenge is especially exacting. Not because the 'real' man was so unlike his image (no one seriously supposes that a warm, benevolent heart beat beneath that gruff exterior), but because that image was so strong – iconic even – in his own time and has been ever since.

The codename 'Stalin' ('Man of Steel') encased Joseph Vissarionovich Djugashvili (1878–1953) like a suit of armour, a protective and concealing carapace. Who the 'real' man within it was is well-nigh impossible to say. As a political figure (which after all is the way he won his fame and how he's been remembered), he was to a considerable degree a construction of propaganda, mythologizing on his own side and demonizing on his enemies'. As such, he represented a set of values and a system of government – for better or for worse, according to ideological perspective.

Russians, then, were encouraged to regard Stalin with reverence as their national 'father'; austere but ultimately loving, a valiant protector of their security and the overseer of all justice in their state. In his tireless efforts on behalf of the Soviet Union he was an inspiration alike to the industrial worker, the farm labourer, the office clerk and the schoolteacher as well as the soldier on the battlefield and the mother in her home.

For the capitalist media, by contrast, his moustachioed visage was the monstrous face of Communism in all its godless tyranny, mass enslavement and repression. (There was, it's true, a brief few months during World War II when, as an ally of the Western powers against Germany, he was affectionately depicted as an avuncular 'Uncle Joe', but this was very much a temporary blip.)

It's tempting to reach for the judicious-sounding, liberal conclusion that 'the truth is somewhere in the middle' of these extremes. But that claim doesn't itself carry conviction. The idea of a 'moderate' Stalin is so oxymoronic as to be immediately and utterly unacceptable. Either of the extreme views seems preferable. And it may be that both were equally true and untrue, and that this ambivalence was key to his significance – his status as (secular) divinity and devil all at once.

Below: All sectors, all ethnicities ... Stalin stands as the People's choice, the People are gently reminded in this propaganda poster from 1935.

15

NUMBERS GAME

'A single death is a tragedy …', Stalin is supposed to have said; 'A million deaths is a statistic.' Whether he really made the claim or not, it contains much truth. But there's truth as well in the earlier, anonymous suggestion that there are 'lies, damned lies, and statistics'. The most incontrovertible 'facts and figures' may mislead.

The paranoia and secrecy of the Cold War brought about a perfect storm of speculation in Western scholarship, provoked by the evident brutality of Stalin's Soviet regime and the clear mendacity of its spokesmen. In the absence of credible countering information, historians and political scientists were reduced to wild guesswork. Reputable historians were to estimate a death toll under Stalin of anything up to 60 million.

Since the collapse of Communism in 1989, however, and the subsequent opening up of the Soviet state archives, it's been clear that these totals were massively exaggerated – even allowing for under-recording in the official files. The Soviet state was nothing if not bureaucratic; nor is there any sign that its executioners felt any doubt or shame, so it seems unlikely that its official records significantly understate the facts. They suggest

Above: The memorial to the Ukrainian Famine, Kiev.

a figure of around three-quarters of a million for Stalin's 'Great Purge' of 1936–8 and a few million more for the Ukraine Famine (which was very much an act of Stalin rather than of God).

That it must have been a terrifying time to be alive in Russia isn't disputed, but Western historians now believe that, even allowing for killings that were

concealed or simply unrecorded, the Great Purge is unlikely to have cost more than a million lives – if that. Likewise, the Famine that followed from Stalin's forcible collectivization programme isn't believed to have resulted in more than, say, five million deaths.

MIRRORING MONSTROSITIES

Already the author of *Hitler: A Study in Tyranny* (1952), the Nazi leader's first full-length biography, English historian Alan Bullock (1914–2004) followed up four decades later with *Hitler and Stalin: Parallel Lives* (1993). Vast and formidably erudite, this fascinating study made a compelling case for the historical interrelation of the two dictators. Their careers had been complementary, Bullock argued, each one had risen to power in opposition to the other's rise; each holding up the other as a bogeyman to be armed against and resisted at whatever cost.

Exhaustive as Bullock's study was, as intriguing as the parallels it identified were, it didn't find extensive *similarities* between the two men. Beyond, that is, the obvious ones that both gained supreme power and committed acts of supreme evil. Both, as children, had suffered under domineering fathers; both had been the victims of what we'd now see as serious domestic abuse – though the same might be said of many thousands of other early-twentieth-century children who went on to lead unexceptionable lives. Both, as it happens, had lived in Vienna at the same time just before World War I – though the ethnic diversity that was to alienate the future *Führer* in the Austrian capital had made it the perfect place for the Russian runaway to go to ground.

In Hitler's rhetoric, Stalin emblematized the threat from a Jewish-Bolshevist conspiracy. Likewise, Stalin rallied Russia behind the banner of national defence. But while Hitler was asking Germans to believe in a laughably unlikely alliance between international finance and Communism (remarkably, a great many did), Stalin was at least mobilizing his country against a real threat. Hitler had spelled out in his memoir *Mein Kampf* ('My Struggle', 1925–6) his determination to carve out a vast area of *lebensraum* ('living space') in Russia, where food would be grown to support a strong and powerful German nation. Having cleared these lands by killing many of their Slavic inhabitants, German settlers would set the few they had left alive to work as slaves. If that dream didn't become reality, moreover, it wasn't for want of trying on Hitler's part. In June 1941, he launched the greatest land invasion ever seen, in Operation 'Barbarossa', determined to lay a hold of this *lebensraum*.

Below: German tanks roll into Russia in the early days of Operation 'Barbarossa', 1941.

A SINISTER SYMMETRY

The idea that Hitler and Stalin represented equivalent evils was taken almost as read during the post-war era – in part because this was the Cold War era, too. Whatever their ostensible subject matter, historians – however rigorous they try to be – are always to some extent chronicling their own times, and these were times in which the Soviet Union seemed a real danger to the West. If Hitler's Holocaust had come to represent an unspoken but generally acknowledged 'gold standard' for inhumanity, an all but emotional need was felt to find comparable crimes to place at Stalin's door.

In the absence of credible evidence from the Soviet side, the wildest guesses could seem convincing. The reality would actually appear to be that the number of people killed in Stalin's Great Purge (750,000-odd) was easily matched by the total for Treblinka (780,000) – just one of Hitler's death camps. And while no one would dispute the savagery of the Red Army's final attack on the German homeland in 1944–5, the number of civilians killed was a fraction of those slaughtered in the Soviet Union by the invading Axis forces.

Opposite: Of the two new blood-buddies, it's Hitler who looks less comfortable: a French cartoonist's take on the Nazi–Soviet Pact of 1939.

Below: May 1945. Red Army soldiers celebrate the capture of Berlin.

THE DREAMS OF REASON

When it comes to his career body count, then, Stalin comes a poor second to Hitler. In so far as he represented the excesses and the evils of the West's Cold War enemy, he's long outlived his usefulness. So why does he still exercise so strong an imaginative hold?

In part, of course, because – in keeping with the 'a million deaths is a statistic' law – his crimes were vast enough for the differences between his and Hitler's to take on an academic feel. Who's counting, exactly, when all is said and done? Nonetheless, however extravagant his paranoia, however wild his rulings, however ruthless his decrees, Stalin seemed fundamentally sane in a way that Hitler never did. The German leader's home-grown philosophy of heroic nationhood; his sub-Nietzschean rhetoric of racial dominance; his dream of *lebensraum*; his concept of the 'Final Solution' – for that matter, the 'Jewish Problem' it was supposed to be the answer to – all these things represented a dramatic departure from the realm of reason.

Stalin, by contrast, can be seen as the Enlightenment's worst nightmare: the un-reason to which reason – pursued uncritically – may lead. That he gave Communism a bad name is neither here nor there, but perhaps he haunts us because his example casts doubt of the darkest kind on the whole idea of

Below: 'Glory to the Great Stalin, the Architect of Communism'. Stalin stands against the background of his rebuilt Russia in this poster of 1952.

collective human endeavour and of social betterment.

On the face of it, by comparison with a capitalism based unabashedly on exploitation and devil-take-the-hindmost competition, socialism seems a decent, caring, sharing creed. How did it come to be so cataclysmically destructive? Was Stalin a monster who wilfully perverted an otherwise benign political philosophy or – on the contrary – was his inhumanity the logical conclusion of Marxism's anti-idealist energy?

More than this: does his example – amplified by the subsequent efforts of China's Chairman Mao (1893–1976) or Cambodia's Pol Pot (1925–98); or even the comparatively petty tyranny of Fidel Castro (1926–2016) in Cuba – call into question *any* attempt to improve society by

direct intervention? Are the conservatives who inveigh against 'Big Government' right? Are we setting out on some 'road to serfdom' when we so much as think of regulating business practices or of electing a social democratic city council? The suggestion seems self-evidently absurd, but the anxiety remains at some level and won't be dislodged; the doubt that lurks at the back of every higher purpose we try to have; the fear that the road of good ideological intentions may lead to hell.

In the West, at least, we're long past the point at which anyone would seriously

Left: A red rogues' gallery. From the top, Cuba's Fidel Castro, China's Chairman Mao and Cambodia's Pol Pot. All were to reform their countries, but at what cost?

STALIN AS SCAPEGOAT?

The Left worldwide remains haunted by the failures of the 1930s, when far too few of its adherents were ready to see the Soviet Union for what it was. Humanitarians all, they allowed themselves to overlook the utter inhumanity of Stalin's state, a man-made inferno in which all

freedom, all empathy, all justice, were burned away.

Yet if the Revolutionary Left only too clearly took a wrong turning in Stalinism, it's by no means clear that any of the obvious alternatives would have been much better. His most celebrated rival, Leon Trotsky,

may have been more nuanced in his thinking, but he was ultimately every bit as fanatical and, at the same time, considerably less pragmatic. In this one, highly specific, sense it seems fair to say that Stalin has been scapegoated, as enormous and well-documented as his crimes may be.

think of sticking up for Stalin's reputation – even (and perhaps especially) on the Left. Those who remained committed to Soviet-style Communism after Russia's violent interventions to put down protests in Budapest, Hungary (1956) and Prague, Czechoslovakia (1968), were widely disdained as 'Tankies', their loyalty to Moscow seen as slavish.

Below: So unpopular was the 'Workers' Party' with the workers that it often had to impose itself by force, as here in Budapest, Hungary, 1956.

Stalin's henchman Lazar Kaganovich (1893–1991) is notoriously reported to have said, in defence of his leader's ruthlessness: 'You can't make an omelette without breaking eggs.' Now, with Soviet Communism no more than a rapidly receding memory in the world at large, we have very little sense of what the omelette was. Stalin is seen as the socialist Tweedledum to Hitler's Fascist Tweedledee, his reputation defined by the memory of his crimes.

THE ROSE-TINTED FLAG
In Russia too, times have changed and memories faded:

here, however, the feeling of forgetting has arguably been more partial, more selective, more sentimental and even more nostalgic for some people. Although few would really want a return to the wholesale purges, arbitrary imprisonments and summary executions of Stalin's Soviet Union, in other ways those days can seem a little more appealing.

The negatives of this relatively recent past having been, if not deliberately suppressed, then at least not actively commemorated, the worst of what happened isn't present to the public mind.

Left: 'Glory to Great Stalin, Creator of the USSR's Constitution', says the slogan. That wasn't what Soviet citizens were saying.

itself: it had arguably saved the democracies of Western Europe with its stubborn sacrifice. The USSR that Stalin had built was an undisputed superpower – a strong and stable state in which (it seemed) all had their appointed place and purpose, and in which the humblest Russian could hold his or her head up with real pride.

THE PEOPLE'S CHOICE

Hence the finding of a January 2015 poll that no fewer than 52 per cent of Russians looked back at Stalin's reign as being, with all its faults, either 'probably' or 'definitely' a 'positive' for their country. As of early 2017, four per cent went as far as expressing their 'admiration' for the man himself. Not, perhaps, the most overwhelming of popular endorsements, but out of an electorate of over 100 million it adds up to significant enthusiasm for a figure conventionally dismissed in the West as nothing more than a monster. Stalin may not have been much liked by the world outside, they reason, but he was respected – or at very least feared. Who would want to mess with a state with someone like him in charge?

In so far as they do remember the Soviet Union's darker side, people are resistant to acknowledging it, for reasons which aren't too difficult to understand. Proud of their country and its accomplishments, many feel a certain curmudgeonliness about being dragooned into denunciation by the censure of the world. The positive aspects (and there were some – even if they partly depend on things being looked at from the right patriotic perspective) have accordingly loomed larger – and the more so as the years have passed and Stalin's reign has grown more distant. As victor in World War II, not only had the USSR successfully defended

CHAPTER 1

'A VERY SENSITIVE CHILD'

A boyhood of beatings did its fair share of damage, there's no doubt, but there was always more to Stalin than his thuggish reputation would suggest.

The little town of Gori, Georgia, takes its name from the gora or mountain in whose shadow it stands and on whose summit a citadel has stood for many centuries. Imposing and interesting as its ruins are, though, they loom much less large in present-day perceptions of the place than does the

Opposite: The defiant stare may be standard-issue for the adolescent male, but Stalin's psychodramas were to impact on an entire nation.

Stalin Museum, which commemorates the community's most famous son.

And most infamous. For Joseph Stalin's reputation has been nothing if not controversial. Any historical legacy is complex and his has been bitterly contested. The debate over how we should see him shows little sign of diminishing in rancour – even now, over half a century after his death. The ups and downs of his historical fortunes, as they have been perceived in his native land, at least, have to some extent been charted in his museum.

AIRBRUSHED OUT

Construction commenced under Stalin himself, and continued after his death in 1953 under his successor as First Secretary of the Communist Party and Soviet Premier, Nikita Khrushchev (1894–1971). A concession to Georgian pride (the local patriotism that dared not speak its name under socialism but was still to some extent accommodated), this went against the grain of the wider culture in the Soviet Union, which at this time was striving to suppress the very memory of Stalin.

Khrushchev was to denounce Stalin in a celebrated speech to the Party Congress, delivered in Moscow on 14 February 1956. It was certainly no Valentine: Khrushchev condemned the late leader's 'personality cult' – and its consequences for the country as a whole. These, said Khrushchev, had included not only the 'execution, torture and imprisonment of loyal party members on false charges' but the near-destruction of Soviet agriculture.

He even took a swipe at what might have seemed the most certain and secure of Stalin's achievements: his victory in the 'Great Patriotic War' of 1942–5. Not only had it been the late leader's mistakes which had precipitated

Germany's invasion in the first place, Khrushchev charged: his purges had almost fatally compromised his country's ability to defend itself. A few years later, in 1961, Stalin's embalmed corpse was removed from Lenin's Mausoleum, in Red Square, Moscow, where it had been installed beside the body of the Soviet founder. The city of Stalingrad – originally Tsaritsyn, but renamed in the dictator's honour – was again renamed, this time as Volgograd. The leader who had in his own

Below: Gori's Stalin Museum makes a grandiose shrine out of a humble home. What the photo can't show is the superstructure of historical irony it has since acquired.

day had rivals airbrushed out of official photographs was himself now being erased from his country's history.

Here in Gori, however, the Stalin Museum had been open and drawing in crowds of visitors since its final completion and dedication in 1957. Its position was secured by Khrushchev's replacement as General Secretary by Leonid Brezhnev (1906–82). He took a tougher line with Party and public discipline, and he was largely unembarrassed by Stalin's legacy.

> *His purges had almost fatally compromised his country's ability to defend itself.*

MUSEUM PIECE

The museum as we see it today is substantially the same as it was in Brezhnev's time, which makes it an exhibit in its own right. And not just the building and its interior – or even the presentational style, as anachronistic as that now seems – but the perspective it offers on what was then a very recent past.

The French philosopher and sociologist Jean Baudrillard (1929–2007) was famously to describe what he saw as the 'museumification' of history in postmodern culture – that process by which once real and living places were elaborately adapted and prepackaged for presentation. In a country whose history over the last few decades has been as turbulent as Georgia's, this tendency has been particularly problematic.

Georgia has been independent since 1991, but the memory of Russian domination in the Soviet era is a painful one. To some extent, however, that pain has been assuaged by pride in

Below: Nikita Khrushchev's Moscow speech may have utterly destroyed Stalin's historical reputation – but it couldn't diminish his historical importance.

Above: The 'Man of Steel' in stone: this bust shows the young intellectual idealist – one aspect of a complex truth.

the historical importance of Joseph Stalin – especially, and understandably, in his home town. Even so, there have been frequent tensions and occasional flare-ups in Georgian–Russian relations that have at times had implications for how the Stalin Museum has been seen.

Below: Inside the Stalin Museum in Gori, Georgia. The posters; the photographs ... Stalin was shrewd enough to understand how far he was an icon, a propagandists' construct.

BANNER HEADLINES

In the aftermath of the Russo–Georgian War of August 2008, relations remained strained for several years. In 2012, Shaun Walker reported (*Independent*, London, 5 June) the presence of a sign outside the Stalin Museum, announcing to the would-be visitor: 'This museum is a falsification of history. It is a typical example of Soviet propaganda and it attempts to legitimize the bloodiest regime in history.'

Strong words, though even then they didn't strike a chord with everyone – not even every Georgian. They certainly didn't with Olga Topchishvili, a museum guide. 'Of course things didn't work out as planned,' she told Walker. 'They were scary, terrible times. Of course nobody should try to hide that.' But, be that as it may, she continued: 'Those banners they have put downstairs, saying this is all lies, I don't like that. They should not try to make us forget about our history. I never tell any lies.' A few years later, they were indeed taken down.

RED REDEEMER

Next door to the Stalin Museum – and the reason for its siting here in the first place – is the house in which the man himself was born. On 18 December 1878, it seems – though Stalin himself was later to claim that he had actually been born a year after this, on 18 December 1879. His reasons for doing so remain obscure. The fact that he did is a useful reminder, however, that his whole life was to be mythologized, politicized and surrounded with an ever more elaborate superstructure of – to put it at its bluntest – lies.

Weird as it may seem, then, there's a symbolic fittingness to the decision taken to construct a colonnaded classical temple around Stalin's childhood home. The additions, incongruous as they may appear to the modern-day outsider, turn a modest dwelling into an imposing monument and sacral shrine.

Above: Stalin's childhood home in Gori – a place of poverty, tears and suffering – is here transformed into an inspirational shrine to progress and to hope.

Godless it may have been, but Soviet Communism couldn't do without the sense of reverence to some higher, more heroic being: for several decades, Stalin was to be that saviour.

MADONNA AND CHILD

Ekaterina Djugashvili, née Geladze (1858–1937) and Besarion Djugashvili (c. 1850–1909) make an improbable Mary and Joseph. Not that 'Keke' (as Ekaterina was known to all) was short on piety; quite the contrary.

A peasant's daughter (her father had worked as a gardener at a stately house just outside Gori), her religious devotion was unquestioning. And it was only intensified by her experiences in life. In particular, by bereavement: what should have been Joseph's two elder brothers, Mikheil and Georgi died in infancy in 1876 and 1877 respectively. When she fell pregnant a third time, in 1878, it was in response to her fervent prayers to St George, her country's patron saint. She promised to make a pilgrimage to his shrine at Geri, north of the city of Gori, if he would help her. Those determined that the dictator should have his Mark of Cain can take comfort from the knowledge that Joseph Vissarionovich was born with webbed toes on his left foot. But nothing was going to overshadow Keke's joy at his safe entry into the world.

Right: Georgian national dress confers a nun-like air on Keke – Soso's mother – which her real-life personality isn't believed to have borne out.

Nothing, at least, until the passage of weeks had left his destiny uncertain. By the time she came to make the trip to Gori, for St George's Day, 6 May 1879, however, a devotion of thanks had become one of supplication once again. Young 'Soso' was weak and ailing: his subsequent recovery helped to underscore both Keke's faith and her besotted love for her young son.

HOLY FAMILY, UNHOLY MESS

Though Besarion ('Beso') had accompanied his wife and child to Geri, it seems to have been as a sceptical and, to some extent, reluctant spectator. Understandably, given the extravagance of saint's-day celebrations in which the more determined pilgrims 'walked' round and round the village church down on their knees.

Though by no means an intellectual or a freethinker, Beso was well-endowed with the anti-clerical feeling so commonly found among the menfolk in religious cultures of this kind.

From the father's point of view, however, it suggests a certain semi-detachment, which can all too easily be envisaged ending up in out-and-out exclusion. Whether or not this dynamic was to be the cause, Beso does appear to have become more and more a third wheel in his own family as time went on. A shoemaker by trade, he was for many years a moderately successful one, making shoes in the traditional Georgian style. He had his own workshop and employed several assistants and apprentices.

As fashions changed, however, his business began struggling and then failing; Beso also began drinking more and more. It isn't clear which preceded which: whether Beso's mounting alcoholism compromised his work or whether hard times (and the loss of two sons in infancy) helped drive him to drink.

Both Soso's parents beat him – his mother seemingly in spite of her conviction that her son

Left: The only photo we have of Stalin's father, Beso, is fittingly indistinct. Beyond his brutality, not all that much is known about his life.

was (as she was later to recall) 'a very sensitive child', though her bouts of violence did alternate with fits of smothering affection. But Beso's attacks were brutal, even by the standards of the time. One, says historian Simon Sebag Montefiore, administered when the boy was four, apparently left him with blood in his urine.

UNSPARING

'Why did you beat me so hard?', Stalin was to ask his mother many years later. 'That's why you turned out so well,' was her reply. His boyhood had of course taken place at a time when corporal punishment was not only normal but deemed desirable, in the spirit of the saying 'Spare the rod, and spoil the child.'

Whether Keke's punishments could always seriously be said to be acts of loving chastisement as opposed to outbursts of temper and frustration we might well doubt. But Beso was becoming the stereotypical male abuser – by turns bullying, brutal, capricious and downright sadistic. By the age of four, familiar with the rough edge of his father's tongue and with the pummelling of his fists, Soso had learned to slip away and hide when he heard his father returning home, concealing himself under a bed or even

Below: Humble but homely – but what the 'museumified' interior of Stalin's house can't communicate is the atmosphere of violence and terror that once reigned here.

Beso's attacks were brutal, even by the standards of the time.

slipping round to take refuge with a neighbour.

'Home', in fact, is an ambiguous term here: for all the architectural pomp with which it is presented now, the birthplace-house can barely have registered on the infant Soso. The rapidity of Beso's slide into alcoholism ensured that they'd very soon fallen behind with the rent and been evicted. Sebag Montefiore estimates that they had no fewer than nine different homes over the next ten years. One way and another, it isn't hard to understand Stalin's subsequently reporting a 'wretched childhood', in the course of which, he said, he'd 'wept a lot'.

'KEKE'S LITTLE BASTARD'

'Where is Keke's little bastard?' Beso yelled as he searched for his son when he came home in a drunken rage. Or was he, really, his son? Was Beso choosing his words more carefully than

ANTI-ESTABLISHMENT ANTECEDENTS

Right: A rebel hero – but on whose behalf? Elizbar Eristavi proved a charismatic but contentious figure.

Beso's own father had been a vineyard worker in the hills to the east of Georgia's capital, Tbilisi (or, officially, as the Russians called it, Tiflis). His father had hailed from Ananuri, further to the north.

Not too much is known of Zaza Djugashvili except that, in 1804, he'd taken part in a peasant uprising and then been bound to serfdom for his pains.

Resistance had been widespread. Through the early years of the nineteenth century Tsar Alexander I had been striving to set his stamp on Georgia and the other Caucasian lands as Russian territory, and the people had fought bravely for their freedom. Not for the first time, though, they were used as pawns: the insurrection was driven by an aristocratic intelligentsia, led by the charismatic Elizbar Eristavi (Duke Elizbar).

Despite its appearance of being a popular rising, and its rallying rhetoric of national freedom, the nobility were to be its main beneficiaries.

Once the dust had settled, they were allowed to keep their lands (and in some cases even have their confiscated estates restored) while the peasants who had fought for them, like Zaza Djugashvili, lost everything.

How much the young Stalin was ever to know of this heritage isn't clear now: it would certainly have served to underline Marx's suspicion of what he dismissed as 'Bourgeois Revolution'.

his slurring, frothing fury might suggest? Were there real questions over Soso's parentage? It's certainly been said.

As Beso's beatings worsened, Keke took young Joseph and moved in with a brother – for her own protection, it would seem; not just her son's. Soon, however, her husband – apparently penitent – had wooed her back. But the violence quickly resumed and redoubled and Keke fled her husband's

home again: this time to the house of a local priest, Father Christopher Charkviani.

Father Charkviani, it appears, had been a family friend for some time before this: had he taken a more-than-pastoral interest in Ekaterina? As pious as she undoubtedly was, Keke was admired for her looks; liked for the liveliness of her manner – and, by the less charitable, censured for the 'lightness' of her morals. Stalin himself was

later to suggest to revolutionary friends that his father had been a priest – how far for the sheer pleasure he took in shocking them, it's not clear.

There were other candidates, in any case: whether by design or just despite herself, Keke brought out the protective instincts in a fair few older men. They included Yakov Egnatashvili, a prosperous merchant in whose house she cleaned, and Gori's city police chief, Joseph Davrichewy. Their concern for the pretty, lively cleaner might have been no more than fatherly and sentimental – as might their (clearly genuine) fondness for her little son. On the other hand, their interest might equally have gone – in some or all of these cases – a great deal further. Beso's paranoia isn't hard to understand.

SCARRED FOR LIFE

For several weeks in 1884, a smallpox epidemic raged in Gori. A number of children died on the Djugashvilis' street

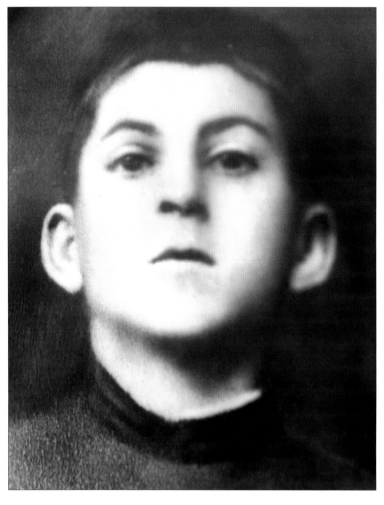

Left: Young Soso's hard-faced stare shows the steel armour firmly in place. Sadly, he was already deeply damaged.

Opposite: The police chief's son David Davrichewy claims to be Stalin's half-brother in this passport document dating from 1922.

TAKING OPPORTUNITIES?

'When I was young I cleaned house for people, and when I met a good-looking boy I didn't waste the opportunity.' Much scholarly speculation has been devoted to this remark, allegedly made by Keke many years later to Nina Beria (1905–91), wife of Lavrenti Beria, Stalin's second-in-command. How far beyond flirtation did Keke take these 'opportunities'? (If she even said this. The Berias' relationship with Stalin was close, of course, but always and increasingly shot through with fear, rivalry and resentment, so Nina's testimony could hardly be seen as disinterested.)

To see Keke, as now we inevitably do, through photographs taken in her maturer years, it's hard to imagine her having any sort of racy past. The Georgian costume she wears in these pictures is largely black and incorporates the traditional *tavsakravi* headdress, which has very much the look of a nun's veil. Such a garb would make the flightiest and most frivolous seem sober.

On the evidence of her later memoirs, that impression is misleading. They are, as Simon Sebag Montefiore observes, riven with 'earthy mischief'. But this in itself is in no way confirmation of any 'lightness' of character – though Stalin himself was

sometimes to hint as much. In the end, it seems preferable to suspend judgement. This is one of many things about Stalin's young life that we can't know. Certainly, if we're to come to a firm conclusion either way on Keke's character,

we're going to be reduced to relying on (at best) contemporary gossip and at worst abuse. Beso as he beat her drunkenly, it's said, used to describe his wife as a 'whore'. Are we, seriously, to take that as evidence?

alone. Soso survived, though the sickness left him badly scarred – the reason, it's often said, for the luxuriance of his moustache in later life.

Add in his small stature – a grown-up height of 1.62 metres (5ft 4in) – and it's not difficult to see why Stalin would have felt some self-consciousness. He was

Opposite: Keke in traditional *tavsakravi* headdress.

Below: This photo from the late-nineteenth century shows the town of Gori spread out beneath the hill from which it took its name.

said to have charisma, even as a child, albeit of a fairly rough-edged sort, but his father's abuse had helped to make him tough and his (understandable) anger had given him aggression – other boys his age knew better than to try to mess with him. The scars from this mistreatment were of course to be every bit as enduring as his pockmarks – and a great deal more profound in their effects on him.

PARENTAL POWER STRUGGLE

Meanwhile, however, Soso had started as a student at Gori's highly regarded and socially exclusive Church School –

thanks, it seems, to Father Charkviani's intervention. (And, it seems, the discreet assistance of Keke's various male supporters and a local aristocratic luminary, Princess Baratov.)

Eager as Keke was that her beloved son should become a priest (and, eventually, in her wildest and most pious dreams, a bishop), Beso was actively seeking to frustrate her in this plan. Though he and Keke had parted, Beso still turned up at intervals between benders – and he certainly hadn't relinquished his claim over their son. On at least one occasion he seems actually to have gone to the

school and physically removed his son, marching him off to be apprenticed as a cobbler like himself. His mother had to plead with her protectors to have young Soso returned.

Not that Beso had relinquished his claim over Keke either. After a jealous attack on a tavern Egnatashvili owned, which left several windows broken, another of her friends, Joseph Davrichewy, tried to reason with him. Beso seemingly stabbed him with his cobbler's awl. He'd chosen the wrong man to push around: police chief Davrichewy acted with commendable restraint in not pressing charges, but he did effectively send Beso into exile, warning him not to show his face in Gori any more.

His business in Gori having in any case dwindled away to almost nothing now, it wasn't a bad time for Beso to move on. He went to Tiflis (modern-day Tbilisi), in whose Adelkhanov factory he found a job, helping to mass-produce boots for the Imperial Russian Army. Whatever other emotions it may have stirred in those he left behind, his absence must have produced considerable relief given his growing violence

Right: Though much the shortest in the back row, Stalin (centre) seems a dominant figure in this classroom portrait from the school in Gori.

towards both his wife and son.

What he himself felt we can only speculate. We do know, though, for certain that he didn't give up in his long tussle with Keke over their son.

BROKEN BONES

At the start of 1890, Soso was hit by a speeding phaeton (a light carriage) while crossing the street outside his school. Not only was Joseph knocked over, but both of his legs were mangled beneath its wheels. He had to be taken to Tbilisi and spent several months in hospital.

In the longer term, this would mean more scarring, to add to the pockmarks on his face; more awkwardness of movement and more self-consciousness. The accident is believed to have been responsible for the problems he had with his left arm: reconstructive surgery left his shoulder and elbow slightly misshapen, and the arm overall a little shorter than the right. (Some scholars, however, have suggested that this deformity was the result of genetic irregularities, while his father's violence cannot be completely ruled out as a factor.)

Ironically, in the immediate term, his hospitalization had brought him back into Beso's orbit. The accident had potentially been fatal – Keke and the priests simply had to tell his father what had happened. Beso was still dead-set against his son being schooled at all – let alone preparing for the priesthood.

Why, exactly, isn't clear. Did he simply want to spite his estranged wife? Or did he feel a manual worker's chippiness about the idea of education? A resentful sense that his son should not be allowed to 'better himself' beyond his father's sphere? Or even a genuine fear of losing touch?

Whatever the reason, Beso took this opportunity of reasserting his rights as father – essentially abducting his son, and getting him taken on at the Adelkhanov factory. Keke intervened with the priests, however, who had young Joseph earmarked for better (or at least spiritually higher) things and the young man was brought back to Gori to his school.

STALIN THE SEMINARIAN

So well did he do in his continuing studies that, in 1894, Joseph was selected to continue his training for the priesthood as a boarder in the seminary in Tbilisi. The experience was to be ambiguous, to say the least. On the one hand, it was in some ways obviously an enormous privilege: the old-fashioned formal education he

Opposite: Seen here in starkest black and white, without the idealizing 'frame' of its museum, Stalin's childhood home looks a great deal more forbidding.

True to form, his father did his best to put a spanner in the works of his seminary education.

---

was to receive from the clerical teachers here was to stand Stalin in the best possible stead as an intellectual, a political strategist and – ultimately – a statesman. On the other, it was stultifying in its narrowness and its profound conservatism. Its staff were Russian Orthodox priests, not just doctrinally but culturally and linguistically, who did their best to suppress any Georgian identity their students might feel.

And, of course, the seminary was run with a severity which went well beyond strict discipline into the realms of outright cruelty. Nor did the tyranny end there. Even by the grisly standards of other such institutions of the time, it was notorious for its culture of bullying among the student body. Tough as he'd already had to be, Joseph had his hands full here – not least because of his consciousness (and his fellow seminarians') of his class status. Again, however, as at Church School, he was to show that he was well up to the job.

It must have felt a mixed blessing for him that Keke had accompanied him to the city,

earning money by working as a seamstress – and, more humiliating for Soso, by helping out in the seminary canteen. He himself had to sing in the choir to earn small sums: despite the assistance of his Gori sponsors, there seems to have been a constant battle to afford his fees. True to form, his father did his best to put a spanner in the works of his seminary education by turning up at intervals and trying to remove him – or simply begging for beer money.

As at Gori earlier, Joseph was unusual in being both a troublemaker and an academic high-flier, handy alike with his fists, his insolent back answers and his brain. He took himself seriously as a thinker and a writer, and, for that matter, as a poet, creating works of real value at this time.

A COSMOPOLITAN CAPITAL

Lacelike railings richly carved in wood adorn the balconies of old Tbilisi, a tourist attraction down through Soviet times to the present day. If at sixteen Soso wasn't really of an age to appreciate picturesque quaintness of this kind, he must at least have sensed the bustling beauty of his country's capital. Under Russian rule, efforts had been made to modernize and beautify Tbilisi – if only to persuade its people of the benefits of their subject status. Some spacious boulevards and elegant public buildings had certainly raised the architectural tone – without, however, really 'Russianizing' the city successfully.

Nineteenth-century visitors conventionally found that Tbilisi had an exotic, even Asiatic feel. With its narrow, winding streets and its busy, souk-like markets, it didn't seem quite like any modern city in Central or Western Europe. About a third of the population was of Armenian descent; there were Tatars, too (from Central Asia), a thriving Jewish community, a colony of German craftsmen and traders, and a significant Muslim minority (many of them Persian).

Though as yet only a small fraction of its present size, Tbilisi was still a sizeable city, and growing rapidly as workers and their families streamed in from surrounding towns and countryside.

In 1865, its population had been 71,000, rising to 120,000 by 1900. Late as the industrial revolution had been in arriving in the Caucasus, it was here now, and creating a good deal of disruption. Beso's drinking might have left him particularly vulnerable in the face of industrial competition, but he'd hardly been alone in the economic pressures he had been feeling.

RADICAL READINGS

Quite how much this ferment can have impacted on young Stalin we can't say. Very little,

Below: From its narrow streets and Asiatic architecture to the strangeness of its people's clothing, nineteenth-century Tbilisi had an irresistibly exotic feel for visitors.

perhaps: he and his fellow seminarians lived in virtual imprisonment, after all. In so far as they were able to see beyond the seminary's walls, however, they could look out at exciting, changing times and on a city that was very clearly going places.

In any case, they were of an age to think of change as not only possible but essential – and of themselves as self-evidently capable of bringing it about. Socialism, anarchism and radical philosophies of every kind were in the air, coming through on the slipstream of a scientific revolution that had been

calling all the old orthodoxies – religious, social and cultural – into question.

It is perhaps surprising to think of such questions being eagerly debated inside a seminary – and, indeed, the priests who ran it suppressed all such heresies as completely as

Below: Grand on the outside, brutal within. Stalin's Tbilisi seminary emblematizes the social and spiritual contract Nikolai Chernyshevsky (inset) was to question in his works.

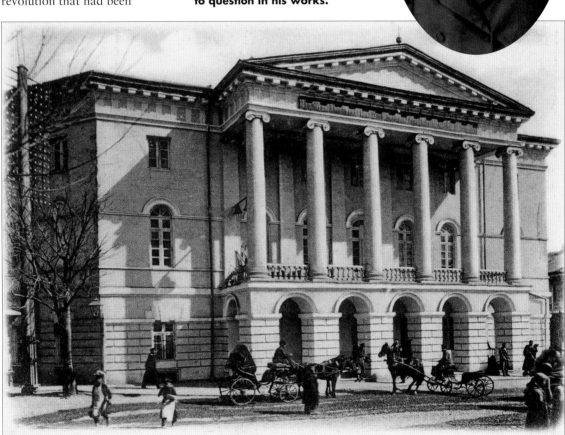

they could. But, however hard they'd tried to restrict its scope, the education they'd given their students had been, first, an attempt to inculcate a sense of duty and, second, a training in how to think. Most seminarians might have emerged from their education firmly anchored in conservative certainties, but those inclined to question those certainties were well-equipped to do so.

Stalin seems to have become involved with a group of students who, with a certain amount of cloak-and-dagger posturing, met regularly to discuss the works of the more notorious nineteenth-century writers. No one as profoundly problematic as Marx, of course, but dangerously free-thinking (and French) writers such as Victor Hugo (1802–85) and Émile Zola (1840–1902) as well as Russian poets like Nikolai Nekrasov (1821–77). Nikolai Chernyshevsky (1828–89) represented radicalism of a rather different order: his state-of-the-nation novel What is to be Done? (1863) was openly revolutionary in its message. Lenin was famously to be influenced by it too.

Right: Alexander Kazbegi and Ilia Chavchavadze (opposite, box) were the young Stalin's two great inspirations: both were Georgian nationalists and both were writers.

THE PATRICIDE

A more romantic streak in Soso was revealed by his passion for *The Patricide* (1882), an adventure novel by Alexander Kazbegi (1848–93). An eccentric aristocrat (and, again, a Georgian patriot, openly unhappy with Russia's overbearing attitude towards his homeland), Kazbegi had for years lived close to the

land – and to its people – as a shepherd. Like Chavchavadze, he represented rebellion of a distinctly nostalgic, paternalistic sort – a world away from the modern-minded Marxism Stalin was so soon to follow. He still stood for rebellion, however; for the high-adrenalin excitement of fighting authority and the accompanying satisfactions that comradeship, love and loyalty involved.

Set among the mountains of northern Georgia, *The Patricide* pits the young freedom-fighter Koba against the oppressive local landowner, Grigola – not just a tyrant, but a willing puppet of Russian rule. Koba's best friend Iago is in love with the beautiful Nunu, who loves him back with complete commitment. She is thwarted from the first, though, by the opposition of her late mother's family, who have brought her up. Prototypes, perhaps, for the *kulaks* who were to be such hate-figures for Stalin in his later life, these aspirational countrymen are collaborators with the Russians and with Grigola. They feel nothing but disdain for Nunu's father, a Georgian patriot and sometime rebel fighter. He's deemed far too poor and low-born to have any say over his daughter's destiny.

By now, Nunu is struggling to shake off the determined harassment of Grigola, who wants her for a mistress. Not content with threatening her, he cooks up criminal charges against Iago and has him arrested and incarcerated. Koba comes to Nunu's rescue. Battling his way bravely through to her place of imprisonment, he is too late to prevent Grigola's raping her, but rescues her and solemnly vows to win her revenge. He springs Iago from prison and the young men flee to find sanctuary over the border in Chechnya, joining the Chechen tribesmen who are still fighting the Russians there.

Eventually, they are able to return to Georgia with a Chechen warband, but Grigola succeeds in isolating and murdering Iago, and Nunu's father. This would appear to be the 'patricide' of the novel's title – unusually, given that the word is generally used to suggest the slaughter of one's own parent; intriguingly, given the symbolic quasi-patricide Koba will commit when, in his grief and righteous rage over his friend's death and Nunu's tragic suicide, he rounds off the story by killing Grigola, his nominal overlord.

Stirring stuff and, unsurprisingly, a best-seller in late nineteenth-century Georgia, but the rebel-in-waiting took his enthusiasm to extremes. 'Koba', a classmate from the seminary recalled, 'became Soso's god and gave his life meaning'. He insisted that his friends call him by the nickname 'Koba' from that time on.

A FAMILY AFFAIR?

In the later decades of the nineteenth century, Prince Ilia Chavchavadze (1837–1907) became the bard for an intoxicating vision of Georgian nationalism. His 'Lines to a Georgian Mother' were celebrated:

> Ah here, O mother is thy task,
> Thy sacred duty to thy land:
> Endow thy sons with spirits strong,
> With strength of heart and honour bright;
> Inspire them with fraternal love,
> To strive for freedom and for right.

How far Keke could be said to have fulfilled such injunctions is of course questionable – and, fortunately, academic. For it's as a father-figure that Prince Ilia enters the Stalin story. As a young seminarian, in 1895, Soso went to see the princely poet-cum-statesman at the offices of the newspaper he ran, the *Iveria* (or 'Georgia'): Chavchavadze read some of his poetic effusions and liked them well enough to arrange their publication. He took to what he described (with a poetic perspicacity that in hindsight seems seriously ominous) as 'the young man with the burning eyes' and to some extent seems to have taken him under his wing.

It's intriguing to think of the part this prophet of Georgian nationalism might (maybe 'must', indeed) have played in the young Stalin's formation as a revolutionary.

Ultimately, of course, he was to line up behind a very different banner ideologically: Chavchavadze's dream was of a Georgia led by its (benignly paternalistic) aristocracy. Even so, Stalin had clearly felt both inspired and imaginatively empowered by the older man: how far was this first nationalistic vision to help fire his journey to the Marxist Left?

And, at risk of getting ourselves into deeply speculative psychological waters: how large did Chavchavadze loom in his subconscious mind *in person*? Did this famously charismatic mentor represent a nationalistic 'patrimony' he had come to find emotionally – indeed all but oedipally – oppressive? If Simon Sebag Montefiore is right in his suspicions, Stalin may quite possibly have been behind the order for the Prince's assassination in 1907.

> *For a few, these discussions sparked a lasting flame – and reading about radicalism wasn't going to be enough.*

A NEW THEOLOGY

For most of Soso's classmates, rebelliousness was to be no more than a passing phase, and one to be pursued only at the most theoretical of levels even then. For a few, though, the future Soviet leader included, these discussions were to spark a lasting flame – and reading about radicalism wasn't going to be enough.

Soon he and friends were sneaking out of school at night to go to workers' meetings in the city. There they would come into contact with grown-up activists already inducted into the revolutionary philosophy of Marx. Joseph's grades were now slipping as quickly and irrevocably as – surely by now – his faith already had. He wasn't putting in the hours any more, either in prayer or in study.

Not in religious study, at least. He was reading voraciously in what was already a substantial and swiftly growing Russian Marxist literature. This didn't just educate him

Above: Lenin, 1890. By the time Stalin was self-radicalizing, Lenin was a seasoned Communist campaigner.

(in its highly specific fashion), it connected him and gave him a sense of virtual comradeship with thinkers and activists across the Empire. And even beyond the Empire, given that so many such writers had been more or less compelled to flee to the West and live in exile at this time.

As yet, Russian Communism's effective leader was unaware of his successor's existence – but, at least to some extent, Soso was aware of his. Although the name

'Lenin' was unknown to him (and that of 'Ulyanov' only more so), he'd read and admired those of a prolific writer whose pieces appeared above the byline 'Tulin'. This was an early *nom de plume* of Lenin: the future 'Stalin' was a follower, then, long before the two men ever met.

A 'SPOILED PRIEST'

It's impossible to pinpoint the moment at which his mother's pride and joy was lost to the priesthood. Glib as it may sound, Soso found a new vocation in Marxism and from that time on he was to follow it with religious zeal. He took the political plunge officially in August 1898, becoming a member of the Russian Social Democratic Workers' Party.

Relations with his teachers were by now becoming severely strained: he was constantly in trouble for everything from insubordination to reading forbidden books. In the spring of 1899, he was at last expelled: it's not completely clear why, though the charge sheet against him was long and elaborate. His situation with the seminary cannot but have been complicated further if it is true – as it was rumoured then – that he'd got a local girl 'into trouble' and then promptly abandoned her.

Whatever the reason for his expulsion, Keke was heartbroken and utterly enraged. For some days, Soso had to stay with nearby friends, effectively in hiding.

LITERATURE'S LOSS?

'Morning'

The rose's bud had blossomed out,
Reaching out to touch the violet;
The lily was waking up
And bending its head in the breeze.

High in the clouds the lark
Was singing a chirruping hymn
While the joyful nightingale
With a gentle voice was saying:

'Be full of blossom, O lovely land,
Rejoice, Iberians' country,
And you, O Georgian, by studying
Bring joy to your motherland.'

This famous poem (here translated by the historian Donald Rayfield) was learned by heart by just about every Georgian schoolchild in the Soviet era. It's essentially a national hymn ('Iberia' was the name given by the Romans to their Georgian province). While its authorship was kept anonymous, it had in fact been among those presented by Joseph Vissarionovich Djugashvili to Prince Ilia Chavchavadze when he went to see him as a patriotic postulant.

Was Russian history's gain (if you can call it that) Georgian literature's loss? It's difficult to say of a poem like this how well it has stood the test of time. All but the most exceptional late-Romantic poetry of the early twentieth century, Europe-wide, reads like over-florid fustian now.

In Stalin's case, of course, there has been much more at stake than chronology or changing tastes. It's impossible for us to read these softly scented stanzas with all their delicate flower petals and gentle birdsong without being reminded of the terror and the misery that were to be its author's more enduring oeuvre.

At the same time, it seems only fair to acknowledge that Joseph Stalin was a real poet (or at least came close to that title) in a way that, with all his pretensions, Adolf Hitler never was a real artist. Indeed, while substantive evidence has not survived, there's a fair amount of testimony to suggest that Stalin was also accomplished in the visual arts in a way the Nazi leader never was.

Not that this in any sense lessens his later crimes, of course, but it does perhaps help change our perceptions of the man. For obvious and understandable reasons, he's since been stereotyped as a simple, straightforward thug. In some ways, indeed, he played up to that image himself. The reality would seem to be that he was a highly intelligent and extremely cultured thug, whose reflexive philistinism was in important ways a pose.

CHAPTER 2

RED DAWN

'Soso' took to the revolutionary life as though to the manner born.
He was short of scruples, maybe, but not of courage.

Just outside the centre of Tbilisi, on the banks of the River Mtkvari, stands what is left of the city's Meteorological and Magnetic Observatory. Built in 1858, it was designed by the Dresden-born Otto Jakob Simonson (1829–1914), Tbilisi's city architect at the time. It was here that, his promising future

Opposite: A portrait of Stalin circa 1900. Young Stalin is a favourite on Internet lists of 'hot dictators'. And fair enough – though his brutal side was well-developed by this time too.

as a priest now firmly behind him, Joseph Vissarionovich Djugashvili found a job, monitoring the weather.

Since leaving the seminary that spring, he'd done a few months' tutoring for local families but barely managed to get by: on 28 December 1899, however, he started at the Observatory.

LOW PRESSURE

As a junior 'observer', his days were long: 6.30 a.m. through to 10 p.m. His duties could hardly be described as exacting, though. All he had to do was take readings of temperature and air

pressure every hour and carefully record them.

In between, he could read or lounge and take his ease. He only had to cover three such shifts a week, moreover: the remaining four days were entirely his own. And if his pay was pretty meagre, his accommodation came rent-free. There was no commute: Joseph had his own room in the observatory itself so simply had to clamber out of bed to be at his place of work.

He also had company, in the shape of Vano Ketskhoveli and Mikhail Davitashvili. Both were sometime schoolmates

Above: A large, semi-casual workforce was needed to keep the Tbilisi railyard running. Stalin found a receptive audience for his speeches here.

– the former since his Gori days; but they were also fellow Communists as well as workplace colleagues. It seems indeed to have been Ketskhoveli – a predecessor on the path from the priesthood to the Party – who had helped secure the position for his friend.

The Observatory had quite the socialist social scene. It wasn't much of a job, maybe,

but in the liberty it allowed him it was the answer to a young revolutionary's (strictly atheistic) prayer. For the real business of Soso's life now was political agitation. Just a short walk from where he lived, in the Didube district, was Georgia's most important railway yard, which he was soon to make his second home. Every day he wasn't on duty at the Observatory, he'd go to the depot and hang around, chatting to the workers between their shifts, striking up acquaintances and making connections. In no time at all, it seems, he had been accepted as an honorary railwayman,

was organizing impromptu meetings and recruiting comrades to his cause.

SUNNY INTERVAL

All seemed set fair as the spring of 1900 approached, but Soso's activities were already attracting attention from the police. Plans were well advanced by now for strikes and protests to mark May Day, and the authorities were keen to nip them in the bud. Joseph had only been at the Observatory for about three months when, arriving home one day on the city tram, he saw officers clustering around it, clearly closing in to raid the place. He stayed on board and rode right past his stop, then went to a comrade's house, going to ground and living in hiding from that time on.

Always, for the time being at least, succeeding in keeping one step ahead of his pursuers, he helped Lado Ketskhoveli (Vano's brother) run the radical newspaper, the *Kvali*. This publication had been founded by the liberal writer Georgi Tsereteli (1842–1900) as a platform for anti-establishment views of just about every kind in Georgia. Now it became the mouthpiece of the Marxist Left and a particular clique within the Marxist Left as well.

The *Kvali* expressed the views of Joseph and Lado as against those of Noe Zhordania (1868–1953). Zhordania argued eloquently for a widening of the Party to include as many workers as was possible. Soso knew Lenin only as a name, if that – but he'd read some of his pamphlets under other aliases – and was already on board with his idea that the Party should be spearheaded by an elite. Democracy was well and good: the masses should be given what

they wanted, but they needed leaders who could tell them what that was. That this view was beginning to prevail more widely was underlined in November

Below: This house in Tbilisi was an important centre for Stalin: between 1898 and 1901, he held meetings of tobacco workers here.

Right: A later and perhaps romanticized view, but there's nothing unconvincing about the forcefulness with which Stalin calls the comrades to order at this 1900 meeting.

1901 by Joseph's election to the Tbilisi Committee of the Russian Social Democratic Workers' Party.

STORMY WEATHER

Within a few weeks, Joseph was off to Batumi, Georgia's second city, sited on the Black Sea coast. It was – even then – a major terminal for the export of oil brought by pipeline from the fields round Baku, Azerbaijan. Soso's energetic, new-broom style helped to galvanize the local activists. For appearance's – and, perhaps, for opportunity's – sake, in January 1902 he himself took a job as storekeeper in a Rothschild-owned refinery. Could it really have been a coincidence that soon after it caught fire?

When the workforce – Communists included – helped to put out the blaze, they expected the usual bonus, but the employers, believing that the fire had been deliberately started, baulked at this. Unfazed, Joseph brought the workers out on strike. At the end of February, after weeks of tension and trouble, a rise was offered and the men went back to work, but management then promptly fired 380-odd 'troublemakers'. Joseph and his supporters saw through this attempt at divide-and-rule and the strike was renewed with noisy protests following. When several demonstrators were arrested by the police, fighting broke out as angry comrades attempted to release them.

The Cossacks were called in: thirteen men were killed and over fifty wounded.

While his traumatized comrades mourned their loss, their new young leader was exultant: 'We may have lost lives,' he insisted, 'but we won the fight.' A rookie red he may have been, but he already understood completely the way

the revolutionary struggle had to be conducted. For the truly resolute, it was a win–win fight: if the authorities were vanquished, that was a victory for the rebels who could bask in the resulting triumph. If the forces of law and order prevailed, that was just as much a victory for the rebels, who could point to further evidence of the oppression

of the workers. This particular 'defeat', he told his friends, had actually advanced their cause by several years. The funeral of the Cossacks' victims, held a few days later in the city, was the perfect opportunity for another protest.

He also had continuing success in the cat-and-mouse game he was playing with Batumi's police, who came exquisitely close to catching him on occasion but couldn't quite succeed. (So charmed a life did Soso seem to be leading that there were suspicious mutterings on the part of some more cynical activists who wondered if he might not actually be working undercover for the law.) His luck was running out, though: the authorities were well aware of his importance and more determined than they'd ever been to capture him. On 5 April,

Below: Stalin leads a crowd of red-flag-wielding protestors in Batumi: organizing demonstrations was pretty much his daily work.

they got intelligence that he was speaking at a meeting in a house in the city. Surrounding the premises, they moved in quickly and arrested him.

COLD FRONT

Imprisoned in Batumi and then, after that, Kutaisi, west of Tbilisi, Joseph took a leadership role among the other political prisoners around him. He contributed wholeheartedly to the general cause, giving classes and lectures in Marxist theory, which didn't just educate but helped maintain morale. He organized protests that won small but psychologically

significant concessions for his fellow inmates. Even so, it was generally felt that he remained in some important sense isolated – at once socially and (still more, emotionally) aloof.

He carried on with such activities after he had been sent to Siberia in the latter part of 1903. Not that he was to be there very long. Condemned to exile, rather than imprisonment, here, he was billeted on a peasant family in the little town of Novaya Uda, Irkutsk.

Any austerity he had to suffer here was, consequently, just the normal hardship endured by Siberia's poor. The punishment

lay in the remoteness of the posting. Joseph, unaccustomed to comfort in his own life up to this point, didn't struggle with the former, but found the latter every bit as tough as he was supposed to. He made determined efforts to escape, on one occasion getting clean away but finally being forced to surrender by exhaustion and by frostbite. A few months later, in the warmer weather, he

Below: Fourth from the left in the back row, a shock-headed Stalin lines up with other inmates at Kutaisi, 1903.

tried again and had better luck, eventually managing to make his way back to Georgia. He stayed with friends and comrades-at-arms like Sergei Alliluyev (1866–1945), a Russian-born railwayman and Party activist.

As comparatively brief as his absence had been, he returned to the fray a tried and proven veteran, with all the

Right: Stalin stands with his second wife Nadezhda, all grown up.

Below: Stalin spent time in this cell at Batumi, 1903.

FATHERLY CONCERN

Olga, Sergei Alliluyev's wife, was notoriously unfaithful in general and was widely rumoured to have had an affair with her husband's younger friend, Soso, in particular. There's nothing inherently implausible about this claim. On the other hand, neither does it seem so improbable that Joseph (or Sergei's) enemies might have made it up: revolutionary solidarity is no bar to personal back-biting, and who doesn't love a bit of gossip, the more scurrilous the better?

What makes this story intriguing (potentially disturbing, indeed) is the fact that Olga was to be the mother of Nadezhda Alliluyeva (1901–32), much later to be Stalin's second wife. If Joseph and Olga had indeed had an affair before, that arguably casts a creepy shadow over Stalin and Nadezhda's relationship to begin with. And this before we even get to the widely whispered possibility that Joseph had in fact been father to the baby girl he was to go on to marry so much later…

extra confidence that brought. His sense of assurance can only have been boosted still further by the fact that, while he'd been in the east, the Second Party Congress had taken place. Lenin's elitist, Bolshevik philosophy having prevailed, the new-look Party that had resulted was perfectly adapted to his talent, energy and impatience.

SUDDEN SQUALLS

Also useful to his cause was the outbreak of war between Russia and Japan in February 1904. The two countries had been sparring for some time. Both had colonial ambitions in the Far East, in Korea and Manchuria. Russia's steady expansion across Siberia had come to take on the implicit status of a 'manifest destiny' for successive Czars and the idea that they might be ousted from the east by an Asiatic nation was unthinkable.

Below: Father Georgy Gapon (1870–1906) led the hunger march of January 1905, which was to go down in history as 'Bloody Sunday'.

This was a naïve view – if to some extent perhaps understandable in a European nation of the time. Japan had only been opened up to outside trade by the Western powers (and much against its rulers' will) a few decades previously. It had, however, been making up for lost time in no uncertain terms. Industrialization, though recent, had been extraordinarily rapid, and Japan's imperial aspirations had developed every bit as fast.

Russia's defeat, in September 1905, outgunned and outmanoeuvred both by land and sea, was hardly surprising, given its enemy's military strength and in a theatre so far from the Russian heartland. Inevitably, however, given the chauvinism of those times, it was experienced as a catastrophic humiliation. Russia's rulers weren't enthusiasts for the sort of racial 'philosophies' then beginning to attract adherents in the German and the Anglo-Saxon countries, but they were racist enough to feel an enormous loss of face.

Meanwhile, there had been fighting on the home front too. Already under strain, the economy had begun to buckle under the stress of war and food shortages had led to local protests across the countryside, while in the cities, industrial workforces came out on strike. The authorities' unsympathetic response went well beyond uncompromising when, on Sunday 22 January 1905, over a thousand hungry peasants, led by a priest, who had marched on St Petersburg's Winter Palace to present a petition pleading for assistance, were killed when soldiers opened fire. The demonstrators had been peaceful and unarmed and there hadn't been the slightest hint of a real security or safety issue. Czar

Below: Stalin is supposed to have directed activities at Tbilisi's Alvabarsk printing shop (seen here in model form), turning out propaganda leaflets for the cause.

Nicholas II had not even been in St Petersburg at the time.

A CLIMATE OF CHAOS

The unrest intensified, eagerly encouraged by revolutionaries across the country, ushering in what is now known as the Revolution of 1905. In absolute terms, the insurrection can only be summed up as unsuccessful, but to the Bolsheviks it seemed that every little helped. The authorities cracked down with frantic violence. In the two years that followed Bloody Sunday, more than 14,000 people were to be executed for supposed subversion and over 75,000 imprisoned or sent into exile. A terrible tragedy for Russia's people as a whole – and, more individually, for so many activists and their families.

As Soso had realized in Batumi, however, each of these little defeats might as easily be viewed as a victory. Collectively, cumulatively, they helped to discredit the Czarist state and accelerate its descent into what Marx had characterized as a 'revolutionary situation'. As far as Joseph was concerned, the sun was shining on the Social Democrats and he and his emboldened comrades were making hay. Every interruption to the normal order was an advance for them, he sensed, like the inter-ethnic rioting that pitted Azeris against Armenians in Baku, costing many hundreds of lives. Those involved would have been astonished to be told that they were soldiers in the fight for Communism, but they'd been enlisted in that struggle, even so.

As for the Bolshevik 'battle squads' that Joseph was forming at this time, they were in the thick of things, stirring up strikes and attacking all the forces of the law. In between, they carried out opportunistic raids – robbing banks to raise funds, breaking into military depots to 'expropriate' weaponry and even printing works to seize materials and equipment for their propaganda.

'THE MOST ORDINARY MAN'

December 1905 brought a first and fateful meeting between Joseph Djugashvili and Vladimir Lenin when they coincided at a conference of the Bolshevik leadership. Originally scheduled to take place in St Petersburg, that proved impracticable when, on the eve of the event, several comrades (including Trotsky) were arrested and the Party paper closed by police. The venue was switched to Tampere: safe across the border in Finland, but a shortish train-ride

SPARKS OF STRUGGLE

Notwithstanding their enthusiasm for banning publications once in government, the Bolsheviks were copious producers and avid consumers of the written word. 'Koba' (it was still very much a pen-name and not just a *nom de guerre*) was writing analytical discussion and exhortatory articles for the Georgian-language paper *Proletariatis Brdzola* ('Proletarian Struggle').

This was printed at 'Nina', the codename given to a tiny clandestine press-shop set up in Baku by Lado Ketskhoveli, Leonid Krasin (1870–1926), 'Nina' Kozerenko, Avel Enukidze (1877–1937) and others. *Proletariatis Brdzola* was the Georgian sister-paper to the Russian *Iskra* ('Spark'), whose title came from a poem by Alexander Odoevsky (1802–39). It had been written in honour of the 1825 Decembrist revolt – the 'spark' which would one day be seen, said Odoevsky, to have started a mighty fire.

Both these publications – and others as well – were published under the overall authority of Lenin. Though exiled by turn in Leipzig, Munich, Geneva and London, he held on tight to his editorial control. The Party press, he believed, was vital in creating and maintaining the tight-knit ideological and organizational discipline that would be needed for his vision to prevail.

for the delegates who pretended to be a group of schoolteachers on a jaunt.

Soso had come to hero-worship Lenin, 'the mountain eagle of our party'. He saw him as a 'giant' – so was taken aback to find him so small. Stalin's own height, at 1.68m (5ft 6in), was diminutive enough to prompt later speculation about a 'Napoleon complex'; but at 1.65m (5ft 5in), Lenin was still shorter. More to the point, he was self-deprecating, modest: in his political resolve he might be the 'Iron Man', of which 'Lenin' was the literal meaning, but in his personal presentation he was unassuming.

As soon as he started speaking, though, Lenin exerted a near-hypnotic pull over his hearers, many witnesses were to recall – not with his rhetoric but with his compelling logic. Joseph, though initially awestruck, quickly mastered himself sufficiently not just to speak from the floor but to oppose a measure put forward by his leader. He didn't, in other words, lack courage, integrity or self-assurance. He still looked up to Lenin as his leader, though.

The conference was exciting, and by all accounts productive. It was only a pity that its delegates were to miss their

Above: A later, Stalin-era portrayal of the man – you can tell by the eager thoughtfulness with which Lenin listens to the young activist.

Overleaf: Stalin, incognito but intense, in 1905.

revolution. Workers' risings took place in Moscow and Tbilisi in the Bolsheviks' absence, and had been brutally crushed by the time their supposed leaders could return to join them.

Joseph got home to find the fight still sputtering on in places, but largely lost, thanks to the savage repression of

A MARRIED MAN

In July 1906, Soso compromised with bourgeois morality sufficiently to enter the married state with Ketevan Svanidze (1885–1907). (Such was the depth of his affection, indeed, that he agreed to have their wedding in a church.) 'Kato' was a seamstress – though not the stereotypical 'poor seamstress' of nineteenth-century fiction: her family were members of the minor nobility. They had, however, come down in the world and lived in (comparatively) genteel poverty. With her two sisters, Kato worked for a fashionable French dressmaker in Tbilisi, Madame Hervieu, helping dress the elite of Tbilisi's high society.

Their father was a schoolteacher; their brother, Alexander Svanidze (1886–1941), had been at the seminary with Joseph. He too had forsaken the Church for the Revolution. It was through him that Soso had come into contact with Ketevan: he was one of several lodgers living in their house.

Her stereotypically lady-like occupation and her celebrated

Above: 'Kato', whose loss in 1907 was to leave Stalin devastated.

beauty notwithstanding, Kato was quick and clever and highly educated by the normal standards of the time. Although she didn't identify as a 'bluestocking', and doesn't seem to have engaged too deeply with the intellectual ins

and outs of Marxist theory, she knew of her husband's political activities and helped him all she could. To the extent, indeed, of allowing him and his fellow-conspirators to work behind the scenes at the Atelier Hervieu plotting the downfall of her employer's client-base. It wasn't long before Kato realized she was pregnant. She had a son, Yakov Djugashvili (1907–43).

When, just 18 months into their marriage, Kato was taken ill with typhus and died, she left Joseph desolate. And, it seems, still more determined than he had always been to take a tough line with emotions and with life. So single-minded was he in his ideological struggle that he hardly seems to have had a moment for any competing interest, let alone for the unceasing demands of fatherhood. Yakov was brought up by his grandmother and aunts. Joseph and his son were never to be close: indeed, Yakov was to find him at very best remote; frequently, he was downright disdainful.

General Fyodor Gryaznov and his Cossack troops. Hundreds of rebels had been killed, along with a fair few innocent bystanders. Soso, it seems, saw discretion as being the better part of valour and urged the people to disarm, but many refused to heed him and the Cossack massacres went on. Their battle squads just about destroyed now, the Communist leaders were left with no alternative but to disband them. Joseph joined with the local Menshevik leadership in ordering Gryaznov's assassination, so that there should at least be some semblance of revenge.

THE EAST END IS RED

A supermarket now stands on the site, at the corner of Southgate Road and Balmes Road, Hackney, London, where a century ago the so-called 'Brotherhood Church' once was. As its name perhaps suggests, it wasn't any ordinary place of Christian worship – neither Anglican, Catholic nor Orthodox – but belonged to a new and unusual denomination rooted in the anarchism of Tolstoy and in the pacifism of the Quakers.

Even so, it was an improbable setting for the motley brotherhood of Bolsheviks and Mensheviks who – putting aside their differences as best they could for the occasion – came together for the Fifth Congress

> *A red-star-studded cast of future Soviet leaders was present.*

of the Russian Social Democratic Workers' Party (1907). A red-star-studded cast of future Soviet leaders was present. Along with Lenin and Trotsky, Grigory Zinoviev (1883–1936), Lev Kamenev (1883–1936), future foreign minister Maxim Litvinov (1876–1951) attended, along with many more. The Russian writer Maxim Gorky (1868–1936) and German revolutionary Rosa Luxemburg (1871–1919) came as well.

The *crème de la* Communist *crème* – men like Lenin, Trotsky and Gorky – were lodged a little to the north, in leafy Bloomsbury; Soso – with the rest of the 'other ranks' – was consigned to digs in Stepney, in the impoverished East End. What this teeming slum might lack in salubriousness, it made up for in safety, however: immigrants and refugees abounded here. These included thousands of Russian Jews, in flight from pogrom and persecution, amongst whom the

Right: Stalin speaks to the workers at Tbilisi's Adelkhanov factory, 1905: he was of course an alumnus of this plant.

Left: Juliy Martov was quickly
marginalized as leader of a
lost cause.

place at another socialist club in
Fulbourne Street, not far away.

INAPPROPRIATE EXPROPRIATIONS

Although the split between the
Bolsheviks and Mensheviks had
taken place four years before,
both factions still belonged – at
least in theory – to the same
Russian Social Democratic
Workers' Party. A state of semi-
detachment prevailed, however,
so each different section had
its own separate meetings in
various different venues, coming
together for joint debates. These
could be unruly, the contempt
and suspicion each side felt for
the other coming to the surface
in ill-tempered shouting matches.

It's often suggested that
the two factions differed in
the violence of their views,
the Mensheviks being more
'moderate'; the Bolsheviks more
'extreme'. To begin with, at
least, this characterization of
their opposition would have
been an oversimplification, but it
becomes more accurate with the
way things seemed to be shaping
now. Martov's opposition to
Lenin's advocacy of armed
action, right away, against the
Czarist state, was couched more
in ideological than in moral
terms – he wasn't primarily
concerned with the prevention

visiting Bolsheviks blended in
with ease.

The Tower House in
Fieldgate Street, the vagrants'
hostel in which Soso stayed for
his first few nights, has now,
ironically, been made over into
a block of luxury apartments.

Soso then moved a few streets
further east to a room at 75
Jubilee Street, which was handy
for the Bolsheviks-only fringe
meetings – mostly held at the
anarchist-founded Jubilee Street
Workers' Club, up the road at
number 165, though some took

of unnecessary deaths. Such a 'putsch-ist' approach, he argued – using the German word for what we might call a 'coup' – flew in the face of Marxist doctrine, pre-empting any popular uprising.

Martov's desire to forge alliances with the wider labour movement has also been seen as evidence of 'moderation' where it was arguably more radical than Lenin's policy, placing more emphasis on the participation of the working class at large. It's true, though, that on both these questions, the Menshevik position did amount to an acceptance of the rule of Czarist law and, as such, could easily be seen as 'bourgeois'.

Likewise, Martov lacked enthusiasm for the 'expropriations' Lenin favoured. In normal parlance, these would be referred to as 'armed robberies': to the Bolsheviks, they were about the workers taking back what was theirs by right. The Menshevik stance against such actions stemmed from this same reluctance to cut corners on the road to

Below: Stalin served some time here at Baku's Bailov Gaol in 1908. His cell was on the upper floor, fourth window from the right.

revolution. Again, though, it was easily dismissed as faint-heartedness.

Be that as it may, in 1907 the Mensheviks found themselves in the majority on this matter and the London Congress voted to end expropriations. The Bolsheviks agreed to be bound by this.

HISTORIC HEIST

Perhaps the Bolsheviks agreed because they didn't want to draw too much attention to operations that were already under way – at least at the planning stage.

Suffice it to say that Soso's very first action on returning home to Georgia at the conference's end was to finalize arrangements for one of the biggest bank robberies in modern history. And one of the bloodiest. Lenin had been involved in the early, big-picture planning – well advanced even weeks before the whole question of expropriation came up for discussion at the London Congress – but Soso's expertise in the detail of preparation and execution was by now acknowledged to be unrivalled.

He was helped by inside information from an old school friend who worked in the mail room of the State

Right: Stalin's police form, Baku, 1908.

Opposite: Simon Arshaki Ter-Petrasian.

Bank of the Russian Empire in Tbilisi's Yerevan Square (now Freedom Square) and a clerk who sympathized with the revolutionaries' aims. Thanks to his contacts, Soso knew that a big delivery of cash was planned for 26 June: it was to be brought

to the bank by carriage from the central post office.

If Soso was well-informed, the authorities were also aware that something significant was afoot. By the time the big day came, then, there was a strong and conspicuous police and

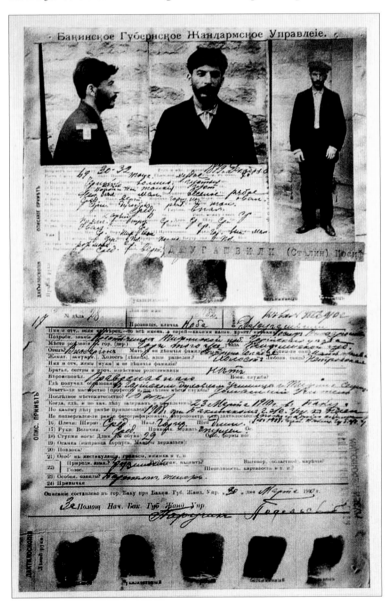

'AN ASTONISHING PERSON'

Some leading Bolsheviks were thinkers first, and revolutionary 'doers' second. Lenin, for example, was a deeply bookish figure. Not that he was in any way especially sensitive or empathetic on that account – quite the opposite – but his cruelty was that of the arid and affectless academic. Something of the same might be said of Trotsky – and, perhaps, of Stalin himself. Both, beside Lenin, looked like men of action, but both had arguably fetishized that side of things with all the fervour of overcompensating intellectuals.

It seems to have been the excitement that inspired him, and the danger that drove him on.

'Kamo' was quite different. Simon Arshaki Ter-Petrosian (1882–1922) had, like Soso, been born in Gori, though the two boys had only met in Tbilisi. Another 'spoiled priest' who had been with Joseph in the seminary, Kamo was in it for the adrenalin, it appeared. Not, of course, that he didn't share his comrades' revolutionary aims, but it seems to have been the excitement that inspired him and the danger that drove him on. He'd caught his seniors' attention early when he daringly

went alone into a crowded theatre and, in the darkness just before curtain-up, threw leaflets from the balcony before the searching police could catch him. In 1903, he'd been arrested and imprisoned but had escaped and rejoined the revolutionaries.

Recaptured in 1906, he'd held up heroically under severe

torture. He was, said Stalin later, 'an astonishing person' who could 'endure any pain' without cracking. He escaped again in time to attend Soso's wedding to Ketevan Svanidze, and took on primary responsibility, under Joseph's direction, for expropriations. At Lenin's urging, though, Kamo's activities were kept at arm's length by the Bolsheviks. He himself scaled back all overtly political involvement at this time. He had his own little team of trusted gunmen and heavies (the 'Outfit') and even a group of Bolshevik-supporting women he could call on to get close to bank employees and other officials to secure much-needed bits of information.

The hero of the 1907 robbery, Kamo fled to Germany but was captured and imprisoned there. He faked insanity – eating his own excrement to prove the point. Sent back to Russia, he was tortured intermittently for another couple of years before escaping again and re-enlisting in the fight. Five years after the October Revolution, he was killed in a road 'accident' (hit by a lorry while out cycling): this was widely viewed as a bit of housekeeping on Stalin's part. His old Georgian comrade knew far too much about the new General Secretary's path to power to be allowed to live and, potentially, cause embarrassment to his leader.

military presence across the whole of Tbilisi's city centre. Soso wasn't fazed: his plan was to attack in such spectacular strength and violence that he would succeed in his goal by sheer overkill. Over 20 conspirators were to be involved in the robbery itself.

Leaving lookouts on nearby corners, Soso's comrades set up an impromptu headquarters in a tavern just across the square from the bank entrance. Soso's lieutenant, Kamo, disguised as a cavalry officer, patrolled the square itself, ready to intervene at a moment's notice if it should be needed. As zero-hour neared, to make sure of having something like a clear run out to their ambush site, they started preventing people from leaving the bar. Even so, the square was crowded with pedestrians as the carriage came into sight around the corner with a company of Cossacks for an escort.

CARNAGE

Masterfully planned it may have been, but the robbery itself relied on the bluntest of implements: Soso's men hurled bombs beneath the feet of the advancing horses. The blast could be heard for miles across the city. Kato was with the infant Yakov on the balcony of

Right: The scene of the crime: Yerevan Square is highlighted in this 1913 map of Tbilisi.

their flat a few streets away. She fled inside in terror at the sound. If the noise of the explosions caused panic throughout the city centre, the impact at close quarters was truly grisly. As passing civilians screamed and ran, men and horses went flying; those guards who hadn't been hit didn't know where to fire in the confusion.

The carriage carrying the money was brought up short, its horses injured – until one of them bolted, dragging it forward. At this rate, the prize might have been whisked away from under the robbers' noses.

But another bomb blew the running horse's legs clean away and it subsided soggily on to the bloodstained roadway: the carriage was once more at a standstill. Soso's men now piled aboard and started flinging sacks of cash out into the back of a waiting phaeton. Kamo came up and helped them load it up.

Leaving the square as they made their getaway, they ran straight into a detachment of policemen, rushing towards the scene. To have come this far, only to be frustrated at this final stage! No need to worry. The ever-unflappable Kamo

simply shouted out to the new arrivals that the money was safe but that they were needed at the bank. It didn't occur to them to question this command from a military officer – a role that Kamo carried off with absolute conviction. They charged obediently on into the square, leaving a clear exit for the robbers' phaeton to ease away with over 340,000 roubles loaded up on board.

Below: Stalin addresses an impromptu meeting of workers on the Baku oilfield.

COUNTING THE COST

What precise part Soso played in the execution of the robbery is unknown now and was disputed from a very early stage. Some accounts had him playing a leading, direct role. A kind of consensus has gradually emerged, however, that, having set things up exactly as he wanted, he stood back and let Kamo carry out the attack. (This is the version confirmed by Kamo himself, for what that's worth.) This still leaves open the question of whether he watched from the immediate sidelines or absented himself completely: again, different witnesses make contradictory claims. Soso could still claim the 'credit', though, for an attack which, when the dust and smoke had cleared, turned out to have left 40 killed and 50 wounded – a dubious achievement, even from the Bolshevik perspective.

On the one hand, it was a real coup, a demonstration of their ruthless efficiency and daring and a real body-blow to the dignity of the state. On the other, the bloody ruthlessness of the robbery had quite naturally horrified the Georgian public. The Communists didn't define democracy in quite the way others might, of course. They were convinced they knew better than the people what the people wanted. But while winning public sympathy wasn't their primary concern, they couldn't afford to be universally hated. The Tiflis Robbery had in some ways come uncomfortably close to being an own-goal.

Especially as the monetary gain proved less marvellous than had been envisaged. Whilst the total haul is estimated to

Below: Stalin's official arrest card, prepared in his honour by the Imperial Police, St Petersburg, 1912.

have been worth in the region of $US3.5m by today's values, much of that money was to prove impossible to use, given that it came in big and readily traceable 500-rouble notes. The $US90,000-odd in easily exchangeable smaller notes was well worth having, of course, but in important ways it had been dearly bought.

AZERI INTERLUDE

For various reasons, then, Soso didn't dwell on this early triumph too much in later life. Nor, indeed, was he to spend much time in Georgia at all. In the first instance, he moved with his wife and son to Baku, where he threw himself into the task of organizing the local Bolsheviks and editing their newspapers. In between such comparatively civilized activities, he got the old gang back together and resumed fund-raising through a varied programme of protection rackets, robberies (several

Secrecy and paranoia are prone to go hand in hand.

guards were killed in the course of a raid on Baku's naval arsenal), even the kidnapping of magnates' children for ransom.

Kato's sickness affected him. Her death in November 1907 completely prostrated him – albeit only briefly: his wanted status had a galvanizing effect. So abject was his state that he hurled himself bodily on to her coffin at her funeral – but he still had the presence of mind to flee before, a few minutes later, a body of men from the *Okhrana* (the Czarist secret police) arrived to arrest him. There was to be no rest for the revolutionary on the run. His luck held for a few more months, but he was arrested in March 1908, and sent first to

Bailov Prison, Baku, then on to Solvychegodsk, in Siberia's Arctic north.

SOSO THE SNITCH?

A few months into this latest exile, Soso managed to escape again. Back in Baku, the work went on, despite his arrest in October 1909. He bribed one of the officers holding him then to let him go. Young, resolute, resourceful – and a great deal smarter than his later thuggish reputation would suggest – Soso had been a difficult man for the police and *Okhrana* to apprehend. And, as various escapes had shown, perhaps an even harder man for them to hold on to. He led a charmed life, it sometimes seemed. So much so that there were beginning to be suspicious mutterings about him. Was he, some wondered, actually in the service of the authorities?

Secrecy and paranoia are prone to go hand in hand.

STEFANIA'S STORY

It was in Solvychegodsk that Soso met Stefania Petrovskaya, a fellow exile. Born in Odessa, into a noble family, she was working as a schoolteacher, though she stayed on in Siberia after her sentence finished and when he subsequently escaped she followed him back to Baku and they lived together. When they

were arrested in early 1910, Soso at first denied knowing Petrovskaya, but after she admitted that they'd been a couple, he sought permission to marry her.

He very nearly did, being granted leave by the authorities, only to be transferred before the ceremony could take place.

Even so, he paid her what in his terms seems to have been the ultimate romantic compliment, adopting the codename 'K. Stefin' in her honour. (To the *Okhrana* agents who at this time had the task of keeping tabs on him, he was known as the 'Milkman', because he operated out of a milk bar in Baku.)

The revolutionary in Czarist Russia was always looking over their shoulder for police spies, and with good reason. The government was keen to maintain the closest possible surveillance on all seditious activities and there were a great many agents and informants about. If they weren't inserting their own undercover officers into the movement, they were bribing or blackmailing the fainter-hearted activists into working for them, obtaining intelligence – or directing misinformation – on their behalf. That way, the Czar's secret police didn't just get hold of vital details of what was being discussed and planned, they fomented division and dissent within the Party.

Activities like those of Soso's outfit exposed the Party to penetration on another front: inevitably, they had to rely at times on cooperation and support from common criminals. If not for operatives, then for information or logistical support or contacts for fencing loot or handing on currency. Such loyalties as the Caucasus' gangsters had certainly weren't to the revolution.

Above: By 1911, Stalin was an experienced and battle-hardened revolutionary and, among the Bolsheviks, at least, a rising star.

On the other hand, there was also widespread corruption within the police and security services: the boundary between government and outlaws was porous from both sides. Hence the paranoia so often noted, not just in Stalin but in all the revolutionaries of his age. Anyone who'd spent any significant length of time in this twilight world of bluff and double-bluff, divided loyalties

THE EREMIN LETTER

The fear and suspicion of the pre-Revolutionary period was to come back and haunt the Soviet leadership in what was outwardly its triumphant ascendancy: it was weakened by division when it should have been at its strongest. The 'Eremin Letter' of 1937 is a case in point. Supposedly written in 1913, by Colonel Alexander Eremin of the Special Section, it suggests that Stalin had been recruited into the service of the Czar's secret police after being briefly arrested in 1906, though by the time of writing, it concedes, he'd severed contacts with the police.

That this missive should have surfaced in the 1930s, at the height of Stalin's Great Purge, is quite extraordinary, given the risks attendant on its wider release. That it did perhaps points to the rage and anger so widely felt during this period, and, maybe, the desperation of the anti-Stalinist opposition. Even in its own time, however, mistakes and inconsistencies pointed to the probability of the Eremin Letter's being a forgery. Since the opening up of the Soviet archives in the 1990s, that has been all but definitely confirmed.

and cold betrayal, risked being driven mad – almost literally – by the kind of cognitive dissonance that could be involved.

Soso hadn't been the most trusting of men to begin with; in later life, his paranoia was to be legendary. That said, if his crackdown at this time was shocking in its violence, his fears were by no means baseless: his party in Baku really was infested with spies. Suffice it to say that he organized what was to be the first of those bloody 'purges' that were to

be his trademark policy – on ever-widening scales – as his career advanced.

As for his own monstrous integrity, that would appear to be secure – tempting as it might be to think of him being disgraced as an informant or provocateur.

And enjoyable as the irony might be in discovering that the man who sent so many to their deaths as traitors, the guilty and the innocent, had turned out to be treacherous to his cause himself, but there's no real evidence that he ever was.

PEACE AND *PRAVDA*

In Baku it was business as usual for Soso and his gang, but even setting aside the risk of capture, there seemed to be diminishing returns. To the outside observer, it had become extremely difficult to distinguish between the high-minded, revolutionary actions of the 'Outfit' and the grubbier expropriations

Below (left to right): Molotov, Stalin and Lenin work hard putting together an issue of *Pravda*.

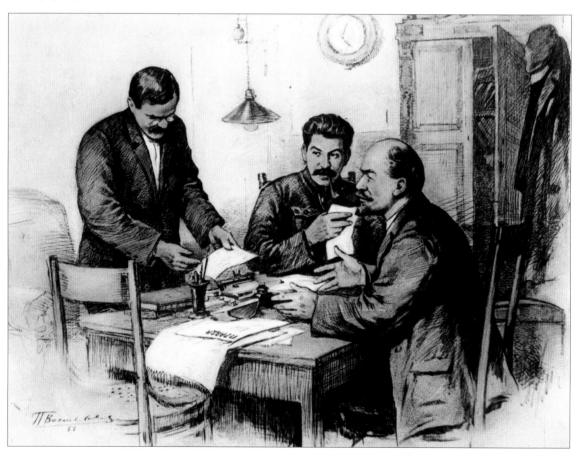

of the more conventional criminal gang. Though by no means embarrassed about this personally, Stalin could see that it wasn't doing anything for the image of a faction already badly damaged by the fall-out from the Tiflis Robbery.

Not that he had any intention of curtailing such lucrative fundraising activities, but with the Bolsheviks feeling their fortunes fading, almost palpably, as the weeks went by, he was keen to build bridges with the Mensheviks again. It was

perhaps his personal toughness and his hardline reputation that allowed Joseph to make this bid for pragmatism when others might have feared to take the risk. Despite his admiration for Lenin, he couldn't help feeling impatience with what he saw as his leader's excessive ideological fastidiousness, and his all too evident taste for petty feuds. The main outcome of Joseph's move was the inauguration of a new Party newspaper, *Pravda* ('Truth'), whose content he was personally to oversee.

EXILE AND ESCAPE

As Simon Sebag Montefiore reminds us, for someone who was supposed to be in the pay and under the protection of the police, Soso served an awful lot of prison time. By the autumn of 1910 he had been back in Solvychegodsk. Soon,

Below: Stalin in Siberia: a landscape sublime in its beauty but impossibly far removed from the centre of political life in Russia.

X (bottom left) marks the greatcoated figure of Stalin, being marshalled with other prisoners for his transportation to another spell of exile.

Stefania Petrovskaya apparently forgotten, he was living with another teacher, Serafima Khoroshenina. In fairness, even if the Bolsheviks had paid more deference to 'bourgeois' morality than they did, fidelity would have been a particular challenge. If life on the run was frantically insecure, life in exile was unpredictable, with the possibility of either party being transferred out at a moment's notice.

Indeed, this had happened to Khoroshenina before long. Soso had been apparently unperturbed. He promptly struck up a liaison with his landlady, Maria Kuzakova,

leaving her pregnant when, in the Summer of 1911, he was moved to Vologda. It's not known whether he ever actually met Konstantin Kuzakov (1911–96), his second son, though he would grow up to be a middle-ranking official in the Soviet hierarchy. In Vologda he took up with the sixteen-year-old Pelageya Onufrieva, expropriating her from another Bolshevik comrade.

In the course of the next couple of years, Soso went back and forth between Vologda and St Petersburg, escaping; being arrested; escaping again; and being re-arrested. He was away in exile at the time of the

Prague Conference (January 1912), but was voted on to the Party's Central Committee in his absence. It seems to have been about now that he started signing himself 'K. Stalin' – not just a heroically strong – but an obviously Russian-sounding name befitting a revolutionary who felt ready to mount a wider political stage. Even so, a few months later, he escaped from Narym by canoe, paddling downriver to Tomsk, and it was back to Tbilisi that he was sent.

Below: This Solvychegodsk cabin was home to Stalin for several weeks in 1910.

But he'd barely been there a month before he was arrested again and sent to Siberia, where he was billeted on a peasant family in Kureika, a tiny village outside Turukhansk, in the Arctic north of Krasnoyarsk Krai. Local girl Lidia Pereprygia was only 13 – well under the legal age of consent – when Stalin's relationship with her began in early 1914. At the end of the year she was to bear him a child, though it died in early infancy.

Another son, Alexander, followed in the early months of 1917, by which time his father was back in St Petersburg with more pressing matters on his mind. One of these was the coming revolution, of course, but he was otherwise engaged in the heart as well, having begun his relationship with another 16-year-old girl, Nadezhda Alliluyeva, his future second wife. Lidia, left without support, married a local fisherman who brought up Alexander as his own: the boy was to learn of his origins only many years later.

OPEN PRISON

The labour camps of the Soviet era were nothing new in Russian history as the Czarist system had sent political prisoners to similar places, under the *katorga* system. The comparison has to be made with care, however – not because the *katorga* was significantly less cruel but because the total number of inmates was so small. An estimated 32,000 people are believed to have been held at any one time, including regular criminals, as against 100,000 by the end of the 1920s – and millions more thereafter.

With winter temperatures in the –40s, and often colder, Siberia was every bit as cold as

Below: Kureika, Krasnoyarsk, where Stalin lived between 1914 and 1916 – for much of that time with Lidia Pereprygia.

advertised. Not that summer was much better: the countryside was beautiful, Trotsky, in 1913 a prisoner in the region of the River Lena in the east, was to concede; but 'our lives were made wretched by midges'. Insect bites weren't just a nuisance, they were at best a low-level torture, at worst a danger: 'they even bit to death a cow which had lost its way in the woods,' Trotsky recalled. With no real effort being made to keep the exiles confined, there was, said Trotsky, 'an epidemic of escapes'. So many, he continued, that 'a system of rotation' had to be arranged:

In almost every village there were individual peasants who as youths had come under the influence of the older revolutionaries. They would carry the 'politicals' away secretly in boats, in carts or in sledges, and pass them along from one to another. The police in Siberia were as helpless as we were.

The exiles' sense of freedom was largely illusory, of course: once outside the settlement, the escaper's problems were only beginning:

The vastness of the country was an ally, but an enemy as

Left: Seen back row, third from left, Stalin sports a hat in this group photo with fellow exiles in a village in Siberia.

well. *It was very hard to catch a runaway, but the chances were that he would be drowned in the river or frozen to death in the primeval forests.*

Stalin himself, we've seen, on his first escape from Novaya Uda, had been beaten back by the cold. As his experience also showed, however, the system was highly porous and determined escapers did quite frequently find their way back to the world.

NATIONAL QUESTIONS

'In Vienna', said Karl Kraus (1874–1936), things 'are hopeless, but not serious.' There's always been a determined frivolity about the City on the Blue Danube. But the home of the waltz was also home, in 1913, to a rather grimmer group of luminaries when Sigmund Freud, Hitler and Stalin coincided here.

One of these people is very obviously not like the other two: the Father of Psychoanalysis was never to be guilty of mass-murder, for a start. But his work on the subconscious, its unacknowledged desires and fears and the sometimes monstrous ways in which these might be acted out was to provide a sort of psychic 'soundtrack' for the history of his time. Adolf Hitler was in Vienna as an aspiring painter – though, twice rejected by the city's academy, and grinding out

For secrecy's sake, he arrived under the improbable identity of one Stavros Papadopoulos.

a sort of living doing postcard-style scenes for tourists, he was nurturing his sense of grievance more successfully than he was his art. He was appalled by the cosmopolitanism of the capital of an Austria-Hungary he deplored as a 'porridge of nations'; the babel of languages he heard around him – and, of course, the numerousness of the city's Jews.

Stalin (though, for secrecy's sake, he arrived under the improbable identity of one Stavros Papadopoulos) was to have a very different experience of Vienna. Indeed, he was to have a very different experience of Vienna than he himself had ever had of any city, as a guest in a palatial townhouse at number 30 Schönbrunner Schlosstrasse. It was here that Alexander Troyanovsky, a noble Russian émigré – and Bolshevik sympathiser – had made his home. For Stalin, it must have been a taste of the high life.

To his credit, perhaps, he seems to have tuned out the splendour of his surroundings. As ever, he simply focused on his work. This time, rather than planning robberies, he

was writing a paper – at Lenin's request – on 'Marxism and the National Question'. A loyal Bolshevik – but a loyal Georgian, too – Stalin must have seemed the obvious candidate to tackle what was always going to be a challenging issue for Soviet Communism.

Marxism was famously 'internationalist'. Fully acknowledging nationalism's role in driving the 'Bourgeois Revolution' that had advanced modernity so much in nineteenth-century Europe, Marx had seen such movements as ultimately limiting. Patriotism was, for him, an aspect of that 'false consciousness' that helped reconcile the workers to the fact of their oppression.

Yet anyone who hoped to establish a new political order over an empire encompassing (as of the 1897 census) 170 different ethnic groups was going to have to reckon with this question. It's no surprise, though, that Stalin's instincts should have steered him towards an answer that involved an authoritarian approach which would build a strongly centralized (and, inevitably, Russian-dominated) state.

Opposite: This commemorative plaque marks the Vienna townhouse in which, for some weeks in 1913, Stalin stayed with the Russian émigré Alexander Troyanovsky.

CHAPTER 3

'CLOSE THE RANKS!'

The October Revolution of 1917 brought the Bolsheviks to power.
They were to wield their authority with savage cruelty.

Today we see Stalin as having been at the very heart of his century's history. At this stage, though, it was passing him right by. While he was romancing little Lidia Pereprygia, World War I was breaking out in what seemed another world. While he was venturing up the Kureika River with local fishermen, or off into the forests with hunters and

Opposite: The October Revolution in 1917 wasn't short of stirring scenes like these: soon, however, the heroism gave way to terror.

trappers from the village, men were fighting and dying in the mud and fire of the Front.

The conflict was already old news by the time, in the autumn of 1916, Stalin was conscripted into the Russian Army, along with a great many other exiles. And, increasingly, bad news. That Stalin and the rest of this rag-tag company of dissidents and criminals were getting the call-up is its own comment on the way the War was going for the Czarist government. It's true that many of the Czar's supporters would have sensed a certain poetic justice in the fact of these national enemies

being forced to fight for the Russia they'd betrayed. From a practical, military point of view, however, such soldiers were likely to be a liability and they'd surely have been passed over had not the need for cannon fodder been so great.

While the Western Allies were just about holding firm (though taking terrible losses) in France and Flanders, Czar Nicholas' forces were having a torrid time of it on the Eastern Front. Ranged against the Russians (and their allies from Serbia, Romania, Montenegro and Greece), the Central Powers – Germany, Austria-Hungary,

Bulgaria and the Ottoman Empire – were making major gains. Morale would have been low in the Russian Army in any case, as its soldiers were ill-equipped, inadequately clothed and fed and ineptly led by officers who seemed in thrall to a corrupt hierarchy.

DIS-ARMED

In the event, Stalin's conscription was quickly to be cancelled. He was discharged as unfit for service, on the basis of the injuries he'd sustained to his left arm in childhood. His Marxist ideology taught him that the war was no more than a power struggle between rival capitalist blocs in which the working class of both sides were being deployed against each other as weapons of destruction.

Even so (and in spite of the fact that no other Bolshevik had been more macho, more gung-ho and more adventurous in his exploits) he seems to have found his rejection humiliating. Many

Above: Despite official efforts, there was no disguising the fact that news from the front in World War I was mostly bad.

of his Party comrades had been carrying the class war to the battle front, calling disenchanted soldiers to enlist in their socialist cause. Russia's adversity, the revolutionaries felt, was Communism's opportunity: Stalin was disappointed to be missing out.

GOTHIC TWILIGHT

What we might call the mood music around Russia's monarchy by now was hardly helpful. The entire institution seemed overshadowed by ill fortune. If, in happier times, the Imperial family had possessed a talismanic status, it now seemed more and more a house accursed.

Emblematic of Russia's desperate plight was that of the Imperial family and court, riven with controversy over the figure of Grigory Rasputin (1869–1916). This grotesque (and grotesquely compelling) character was purportedly a priest, but boasted of supernatural powers of healing. The real miracle workers were his eyes, which gazed into his interlocutor's with blazing intensity and in

Below, left: Rasputin with the Romanov family; right: following his bloody murder.

many cases left them powerless to resist. A drunk, a boastful gossip, squalid seducer (and rumoured rapist) and an all-round charlatan, he attracted publicity of exactly the wrong kind.

Even so, the Empress Alexandra (1872–1918) was utterly besotted with him – not, it seems, sexually or romantically (though there were dark mutterings) but because she believed his claims that he could cure her ailing son. The Czarevich Alexei (1904–18) had haemophilia, a condition that leaves the blood unable to clot and wounds to heal. The hereditary nature of Alexei's illness and its location in those very veins that conferred his royal status helped underline the general sense of dynastic doom. It also, consequently, made Rasputin's influence seem not just baneful but vampiric, adding

to the increasingly gothic aura around the Romanovs.

Alarmed at the damage he was doing the regime, in December 1916 a group of nobles set out to assassinate him. They first plied the priest with poisoned cakes, which he ate apparently unharmed. When he was then shot in the chest and failed to fall, their terror only mounted, though a further two shots did finally bring him down. They pushed his body through a hole in the ice into a frozen-over river.

The story of Rasputin's refusal to die quite naturally took on legendary proportions, his unnatural strength an omen of awful menace for an imperial dynasty seemingly destined to die itself. In hindsight, his semi-mythic 'bogeyman' status helped set the psychological scene for the all but apocalyptic chapter of the events of 1917.

There were still to be consolations, though. Conscription had removed him from Kureika, and the increasingly irksome and embarrassing proximity of Lidia Pereprygia, who was expecting Alexander by this time. Although he was forced to complete his period of exile, he was allowed to stay in the comparative comfort and urban bustle of Achinsk, a significantly sized town in the west of Krasnoyarsk Krai – that much more lively, and that much closer, to St Petersburg. St Petersburg had been hastily renamed 'Petrograd' in 1914 by a government embarrassed by the Teutonic-sounding name it had been given by its builder, Czar Peter I. 'Peter the Great' (1682–1725) had called it this at a time when all things German seemed to have a futuristic sheen. The future as of February

Some 700,000 had fallen at the front; a further quarter of a million brought home wounded.

1917, seemed to be one of revolution.

Russia's capital had been in chaos for some time. The military situation had gradually been getting worse and worse. Some 700,000 Russians had fallen at the front while a quarter of a million more had been brought home wounded with no real way of supporting themselves in an economy that was simultaneously stagnant and dangerously unstable.

Food shortages had been hitting hard. Workers were angry at the exploitation they faced and the conditions they were forced to work in. Tired of being blackmailed into working on by talk of patriotism, they were starting to rebel. Wildcat strikes were called at will and disputes with management flared up at the slightest spark: Russian industry was plunging into crisis. In desperation, the Czar stepped down. As ineffectual as he'd come to seem, the space he left was still more dangerous.

A provisional government now came to power (or to an approximation of it, at any rate) in what became known as the February Revolution. But the Bolsheviks refused to recognize the new regime. Lenin came home from exile in Western Europe to lead resistance. His supporters turned out in their thousands to give him a hero's welcome at Petrograd's Finland Station. Stalin made a quieter entrance, back from his internal exile. He stood for the Party's Central Committee and was

Left: The horizon is still lined with trees, but as its railway station shows, Achinsk was a real town – with real connections to the world.

elected. In between organizing demonstrations he picked up the reins at *Pravda*. As long as he was fighting, he was as comfortable with the pen as with the sword.

DIFFERENCE AND DISCIPLINE

As always, though, Stalin's instinct for unity and discipline in the Party was well to the fore. In a time of thrilling

Below: The February Revolution would eventually come to feel like a dress rehearsal; at the time, though, it seemed real enough.

intellectual and political ferment, he called for the ideological hatches to be battened down. 'Close the Ranks!', he urged, in a polemic that July. In a profoundly puzzling way, indeed, that fanatical intolerance which underpinned all Stalin's ideological assumptions and political actions seems to have stemmed from his having a better insight into the variety of

Below: In this artwork Stalin makes a speech – and his bid to go down in the revolutionary annals as one of the Bolshevik heroes of October 1917.

experiences and opinions than the majority of his comrades. For one thing, as we've seen, he was Georgian, rather than Russian – had, indeed, been shaped by Georgia's nationalist myths, and their expression in the literature of his native land. The Russian majority among the Bolsheviks simply wouldn't have seen the need to (in the modern phrase) 'check their privilege': it took an outsider to see the sort of entitlement they had.

'Marxism and the National Question' had shown how full Stalin's awareness was that what the outside world saw as 'Russia' was actually a tapestry of nations, all jostling for recognition and respect. What he took from this awareness, though, was his conviction that a greater Russian identity had to be accepted – imposed if necessary. If it wasn't, he feared, the centrifugal force these competing patriotisms produced might end up pulling the whole Soviet project apart.

Part of what makes Stalin seem so sinister now is our sense that his totalitarian single-mindedness sprang precisely from this appreciation of life's variety. His intractability and his tunnel vision were born of a deep understanding of the possibility of other views. In a way that Lenin and Trotsky never could be, in other words, he was a liberal *manqué*. He feared freedom, because he

knew – and in his own way valued – what it meant. A similar paradox underlies the point to be made much later, at the height of Stalin's dictatorship, by the writer Osip Mandelstam (1891–1938): 'Only in Russia is poetry respected: it gets people killed.'

Hence the limitations of our later perceptions of a thuggish, philistine Stalin. They're not just mistaken but they let him off the moral hook. Stalin's anti-intellectualism was an intellectual position and he didn't have the excuse of stupidity; in suppressing poetry, he suppressed the poetic side of his own self. 'True conformity is possible only in the cemetery,' he had written in *Pravda* in 1912, in what might easily be taken for a defence of free expression. No one guessed back then the lengths to which Stalin was subsequently to go to make the Soviet Union the kind of cemetery in which such conformity could be achieved.

A LONG, HOT SUMMER

In July 1917, the Provisional Government collapsed. The Bolsheviks were part of the informal Leftist coalition that brought it down. Stalin stayed behind his desk at *Pravda*, cheering from the sidelines, for the most part, but when Alexander Kerensky (1881–1970) took power, the Bolsheviks began to fear for their safety.

Kerensky was by any normal standards a socialist, seeking collective ownership of the economy and government by workers' councils (or *soviets*, in Russian). But he hadn't signed up to Lenin's programme, so they refused to back him. The new prime minister, for his part, saw the Bolsheviks as an obstacle to compromise and

peace, and their leader, Lenin, as a public enemy.

Stalin's experience on the wrong side of the law made him the perfect person to keep Lenin out of reach of the authorities and he moved him from hideout to hideout over a period of days. Lenin's leadership was crucial to the Bolsheviks – not only because of his strategic and ideological intelligence but because he'd come to have a real talismanic status. Whatever differences Stalin might have over minor details of doctrine, he knew that Lenin had to be protected.

In the end, he had no alternative but to pack his leader off to Finland to lie low and see out what threatened to be the last, disastrous weeks of the Bolsheviks' brief history. His role in what was to turn out to have been a decisive period for the Party had been an ancillary one – but vitally important.

Below: In power, however briefly, Kerensky (second from right) sits in discussion with government colleagues, 1917.

LOVE ON THE LEFT

One of Stalin's ports of call during his days on the down-low with Lenin was the apartment of Olga Alliluyeva. He stayed there himself for days at a time after Lenin's departure. Olga was getting on in years, but her daughters Anna and Nadezhda (or Nadya) were now in their late teens and very nearly women.

Simon Sebag Montefiore suggests the possibility that, after so many years on the run, Stalin was drawn to the lively domesticity of the Alliluyeva household. He quotes a source who says that Nadya reminded him of the life he'd had with Kato – dead for just about a decade now. Their relationship probably began this summer, though they weren't to go public as a couple till ten months later, and actually to marry in March 1919.

Actually, Nadya wasn't quite the little homemaker she might initially have seemed. She had a stubborn streak, a strong sense of personal self-reliance and a burning conviction of her revolutionary calling. Not that these would have put Soso off. Quite the contrary, indeed, as there's no evidence that he wanted a doormat, though with Nadya he was arguably to get more than he'd bargained for. Nadya's often vehement political disagreements with her husband were to be underlined and amplified by the moods attending on her bipolar disorder. She was to shoot herself after one such fight, in 1932.

Right: Stalin and Nadezhda take time out to share a picnic with friends in the summer of 1921.

AUTUMN OF THE CZARS

The opposition to Kerensky's government didn't come only from the Left. In September, General Lavr Georgiyevich Kornilov (1870–1918) led a group of military officers in what amounted to an attempted coup. So big and well-organized were the workers' militias that had by now been put together by the Bolsheviks, however, that Kornilov's putsch fell more or less completely flat. It was positively counterproductive, indeed, prompting the return to Russia of an emboldened Lenin and the mass mobilization of the Bolsheviks and their supporters. On the brink of oblivion just days before, the Bolsheviks seemed suddenly resurgent – thanks to a right-wing backlash against democracy.

As the editor of *Pravda*, Stalin had an important part to play at this historic moment, though it should have been very much behind the scenes. Instead, Kerensky's forces coming to his office to smash up his printing equipment put Stalin right in the revolutionary front line. Meanwhile, with victory almost within their grasp – but defeat only a hair's breadth away as well – the task of keeping Lenin safe was more crucial and more challenging than ever.

Meanwhile, on the streets of Petrograd, events were moving on at a dizzying pace and with a truly epic sweep.

With covering fire from the cruiser *Aurora*, whose crew had mutinied against their officers, the Bolsheviks marched on the Czar's Winter Palace, where Kerensky's government were at that moment under siege. His moment in the limelight already over, Kerensky himself had already escaped. He was never destined to return to the country he'd so briefly led. Nicholas II and the Imperial Family had been moved east to Tobolsk in

the Bolsheviks' bid for power. Their view that so deliberate a precipitation of events was not just undesirable but arguably even anti-revolutionary had of course been the original basis of the Social Democratic Workers' Party's split. Now, accordingly, they left the Congress of Soviets, walking out in protest. A contemptuous Trotsky told them they were flouncing off into the 'dustbin of history' – a phrase which has, ironically, become historic in itself.

And so, to all intents and purposes, they were. The way had been left clear for the Bolsheviks to set themselves up as Russia's government. They were not unmindful of the force of the Mensheviks' objections, though; hence Lenin's insistence on a face-saving formula by which, taking advantage of an already scheduled Congress of Workers' and Soldiers' Deputies from across the whole of Russia, they could be 'asked' by the people's representatives to take control.

SHAKING THE WORLD
American journalist John Reed (1887–1920) was famously to call his eyewitness account

Events were moving on at a dizzying pace and with an epic sweep.

the Urals some weeks before – as much for their own safety as in punishment. As the months went by, though, that view was going to change.

The Mensheviks were almost as upset as Kerensky was at

of the October Revolution *Ten Days that Shook the World*. The title did justice both to the colossal scale and the dizzying speed with which events unfolded.

Even before the dust had settled and the chandeliers of the Winter Palace stopped shaking, Russia's agrarian and industrial economies had been formally seized by the state. As radical as this might seem to the outside world – especially, of course, those elements in it with a stake in land and capital – it was no more than Russian socialists had long demanded. More controversial, even on the Left, was the revelation that – the revolution being too important to be left to the people – the Bolsheviks were planning on a Party dictatorship.

Even then, criticism on the Russian and international Left was comparatively muted – not, in fact, because this disregard for democracy was widely shared. Rather, as historian Robert Service was to point out, such questions seemed academic. First, because the sheer abruptness with which all this change had come about had left interested commentators no time to take the situation in, let alone come up with a considered opinion or critique. And second, because no one expected the Bolsheviks to be in power for any length of time.

Not even Lenin, it sometimes seemed: the frantic pace of his Red reforms seems to have been driven by his doubts as to how long he would be there to make them. The more he could do now, the harder it would be for a successor to reverse it all.

Below: Lenin rallies the Party faithful on the eve of the storming of the Winter Palace.

THE PEOPLE AND THE PEOPLES

In other areas, things moved more slowly: it wasn't until 3 March 1918, that representatives of the newly established Soviet Union signed the Treaty of Brest-Litovsk, extricating Russia from World War I. This was at the price of giving up the Baltic states, the Ukraine and much of the Caucasus to the Central Powers – but then the Bolsheviks had nothing invested in the idea of 'imperial' might.

Nor, as we have seen, were they all that comfortable with the idea of nationalism in general, despite having their own Georgian on tap. Stalin's appointment as 'People's Commissar for Nationalities' was another attempt to find some resolution for what Lenin and his fellow revolutionaries knew was a challenging problem for them, both intellectually and politically. That said, Stalin's 'solution' to the problem wasn't especially sophisticated or elegant: the nations should fall into line, he effectively argued, or they should be forced to.

This was of a piece with Stalin's solutions to all the various political and social challenges the Soviet Union faced: it was for the Revolution to command and for the people to comply. Given his subsequent history, it's no surprise to find that he was eager in his support

Above: Felix Dzerzhinsky (1877–1926), centre, and other leaders of the _Cheka_ prepare to unleash 'Red Terror', December 1917.

for Lenin's foundation (in December 1917) of the _Cheka_ secret police and the closing down of all but the Party press.

That said, it's important to bear in mind that much of what was later to be denounced as 'Stalinism' was present in the Soviet Union from the very first. In this period of his political career, at least, Stalin cannot justly be seen as any more brutal than the Lenin who had called for 'War to the death against the rich and their hangers-on, the bourgeois intellectuals; war on the rogues, the idlers and the rowdies!' Or, for that matter, as any more ruthless than the Trotsky who prided himself in identifying with the Father of the French Revolutionary Terror, Maximilien Robespierre (1758–94).

'NO MERCY'

Stalin's differences with Trotsky, especially, were real, and, increasingly, personal, but they hinged on detailed differences over ideology and tactics. They were united in their disdain for humanitarian concerns and in the enthusiasm with which they supported what the Bolsheviks themselves described as the 'Red Terror'.

After an assassination attempt upon Lenin in August 1918, the Soviet leader ordered a crackdown on opposition movements in the country. This was to encompass 'enemies of the people' of both Right and Left (Lenin's would-be killer is believed to have been an anti-Bolshevik socialist, Fanni Kaplan (1890–1918)). 'No mercy to the enemies of the people,' Lenin demanded … and none was shown. At least 100,000 people were executed and hundreds of thousands sent to Siberia. Again, the cruelty of others doesn't diminish Stalin's guilt in any way, but any idea that he made Soviet socialism oppressive is simply laughable.

Left: Fanni Kaplan tried to assassinate Lenin in 1918.

WHITE WAR

In fairness, the 'enemies of the people' were real – or, at least, the enemies of Lenin were. The Red Terror may have been both massively immoral and utterly excessive but it wasn't quite gratuitous. As we've seen, the threat came from both Left and Right. If the opposition of radical socialists like Fanni Kaplan was more irksome and embarrassing than realistically menacing, the threat from the 'Whites' – an ad hoc coalition of the soft-Left, the Centre and the Right was more formidable by far.

In the absence of a Czar, the Imperial Russian Army had lost its reason for being and so, since that February, had been falling apart. Many soldiers, proletarian by background, threw in their lot with the Bolsheviks readily enough; others were forced into it by the violent zeal of the government's Red Guards. The government having been quick and effective in making itself master of the main arsenals and depots, the resulting Red Army was impressively well armed.

Meanwhile, however, higher-ranking officers had largely gravitated to the oppositional force – now known as the 'Whites'. Armies are almost by definition authoritarian institutions – they have to be; their leaders are always liable to display a greater than usual respect for rank and tradition and a conservative cast of mind. Some of the White leadership may have been superannuated 'Colonel Blimps', but they had Russia's most skilled and experienced officers on their side.

With just over 2 million men under arms, the White Army wasn't that much smaller than the Red (which was in the region of 2.5 million-strong). It was assisted, at crucial points, by the

Opposite: The signing of the Treaty of Brest-Litovsk saw the Soviet Union's exit from World War I.

intervention of foreign friends – the British sent an expeditionary force around the Northern Cape of Norway to Murmansk; the French dispatched one via the Dardanelles to the Black Sea and Odessa. The Whites were handicapped by their disunity, though: their army included factions which were fighting for everything from the restoration of the monarchy, with imperial sway for Russia and the Orthodox Church, to democratic liberalism and even 'moderate' socialism. True, their fear and hatred of the Bolsheviks was an important bonding factor, but great gulfs of incomprehension and suspicion still remained.

And that ideological divergence between them was matched by a geographical dispersal that left them spread too thin for optimum effectiveness over enormous areas of Russia.

There were, then, strengths and weaknesses on both sides. The opposing forces were well-matched, not just in strength but

POST-IMPERIAL

The Bolsheviks were able to take a little of the pressure off themselves by signing the Treaty of Brest-Litovsk (3 March 1918) with the Central Powers. Not only did this extricate a struggling Soviet Union from the nightmare of World War I but it stacked the odds against the capitalists' enemies in the West: Britain and France.

Not that it didn't involve catastrophic concessions on the Soviet side – they had to hand over the Baltic states, Belarus and much of the Ukraine to Germany and parts of the southern Caucasus to the Kaiser's Ottoman ally. They had also to renounce Russian claims over Finland and much of Poland. As Trotsky himself pointed out in a bitter communication, the Soviet Union would be signing away 150,000 square km (57,000 square miles) of territory.

Desperate times call for desperate measures – and few have been more desperate than the Bolsheviks' agreement here. They could of course take some consolation from their faith that they were leading the workers of the world by their example, not by imperial force, and that the peoples of those countries would soon rise up to join them of their own free will.

in commitment (and, at times, in cruelty: both sides were guilty of atrocities). The Civil War was bitterly hard-fought.

PERSONAL DIFFERENCES

Almost as acrimonious, however, was the growing rivalry between Stalin and Trotsky over the strategy and conduct of the war. (And, let's be honest, personal differences as neither man was egotistically under-endowed and both were vying for the favour of Lenin.) Stalin was marginalized to some extent as Trotsky was overall commander of the Red Army and, if truth be told, despite his bookish reputation, seemed on the whole to be doing a credible job. Stalin, his trademark paranoia to the fore, disapproved of his readiness to recruit officers who'd defected from the Whites

as 'military specialists' in the service of the Revolutionary cause – though in other ways he was more pragmatic than Trotsky was.

Where he was given scope to do things the Stalin way, in southern Russia, he gave – as historian Robert Service has said – a foretaste of what was to come in the 1930s. No sentimentalists themselves, Lenin and Trotsky both seem to have been taken aback by the energy with which, sent to take charge of things in southern Russia, where troops had been deserting and defecting in vast numbers, Stalin rounded up alleged 'counter-revolutionaries' and had them summarily – and very publicly – executed by firing squads. No respecter of anyone's authority but Lenin's (and not always of his), he took it upon

himself to purge the military specialists set to supervise the assembly and distribution of supplies in Tsaritsyn (subsequently Stalingrad, now Volgograd), many of whom were to be executed on his orders too.

Nor were the civilian population to be spared. Stalin had whole villages burned down at the merest hint of resistance, an exemplary punishment from which neighbouring communities could learn. Again, his comrades, ruthless as they

Opposite: Spartacists march in Germany, inspired by the Bolsheviks' example.

Below: The saviours of their nation or its triumvirate of terror? Stalin, Lenin and Trotsky, 1919.

RED FLAG FLYING

History wasn't to bear out the Bolsheviks' expectations of a world- (or at least a Europe-) wide revolution. Even so, they weren't wholly unreasonable at the start. Germany's defeat in 1918 sparked serious and widespread unrest, beginning with a mutiny of naval sailors. The Kaiser's abdication came in response to the Revolution's spread, but the rebels disagreed over how extensive reform should be. Dissatisfaction with the more 'moderate' programme of the Social Democratic Party led to a sort of revolution-within-a-revolution with the Soviet-style 'Spartacist' revolt of January 1919. The brutal manner of its suppression cast a pall of suspicion and resentment over the entire course of the Weimar Republic.

Modern, go-ahead Germany had been marked out by Marx as an obvious centre for revolutionary developments. So too had the first of the industrial powers, Britain. There, indeed, the Russian Revolution was to prove inspirational to the militant working class, prompting waves of strikes, protests and rioting from London's East End to Liverpool. 'Red Clydeside' saw what was widely believed to be the beginnings of a socialist state in Glasgow before this was successfully put down by the authorities.

The Russian Revolution also inspired an upsurge in labour activism in the United States – though this was dwarfed in scale and rhetorical intensity by the 'Red Scare' it produced among politicians of the Right. Given America's unique history, and its associated prejudices, 'Reds' and 'Blacks' became closely identified in the conservative mind: 1919 saw a summer-long spate of lynchings.

were, seem to have been shocked by Stalin's sheer brutality and his readiness to use terror as a means of political control.

The Whites were by no means innocent, as serious pogroms were mounted in territories that they controlled. By 1919, the structural challenges the Whites had to contend with had proven insurmountable and the Red Army very clearly had the upper hand. Their hold was not as yet secure though; in the south, especially, the Whites remained present in some strength.

The Bolsheviks, only a year or so ago on the edge of annihilation were now not only running Russia but looking to lead a revolutionary movement far beyond.

There was growing confidence that Western labour movements, inspired by what was being achieved in Russia, would rise up and bring the rest of Europe to their side.

PROBLEMS IN POLAND

Clashes over areas disputed between Soviet Russia and Poland flared up into full-on war in 1919. Lenin and Trotsky welcomed the conflict as a chance to spread the revolutionary word. But Stalin – perhaps showing signs of that instinctive caution that was later to issue in his philosophy of 'Socialism in One Country' – seems to have been more sceptical. He had been reluctant to celebrate a Bolshevik 'victory' in the Civil War while the Whites remained a presence in the south and didn't see that the Soviet Union needed to be taking on new enemies on other fronts just now.

Even so, he did his duty, leading the army besieging the city of Lwow (now Lviv, in western Ukraine). Once again, though, he was seriously at

Below: The Poles administered an early humiliation to revolutionary Russia when, in 1920, they defeated them; here, volunteers line up armed only with scythes.

Above: Soviet troops set out for the Polish front.

odds with Trotsky. It appears to have been on Lenin's orders that Stalin and his forces failed to respond to Trotsky's summons to assist his main Red Army force at the Battle of Warsaw (August 1920), but the Red Army commander became convinced that Stalin had slighted his orders deliberately.

If not simply to spite him, Trotsky reasoned, it had been to gain more personal glory at Lwow. He accused his rival of insubordination. Stalin looked to Lenin for support, only to find himself left hanging. He himself requested that he be dismissed from military service.

A low point in Stalin's political career, then: it didn't seem to make things any better that this was already clearly a low point in the Soviet state's short history. The Polish won, and although those territorial concessions made under the Peace of Riga (1921) were viewed as hopelessly insufficient by Polish nationalists, they were experienced as a real humiliation by the Russian side. Worse, however, for Lenin was the realization that Poland, in standing firm, had placed a seemingly-insurmountable barrier between the Soviet Union and its projected political

expansion towards the West. For Stalin, this chapter in Soviet history ended equivocally. He'd been humiliated – in some circles, even, apparently disgraced. On the other hand, he'd been vindicated in his judgement – not just on the desirability of war with Poland, but on the whole idea of 'exporting revolution' to the wider world. His instinct to consolidate, to 'close the ranks', had been borne out by what had now happened.

Вся власть советамъ!

1917   1934
ВЫШЕ ЗНАМЯ ЛЕНИНА—
ОНО НЕСЕТ НАМ ПОБЕДУ!

Да здравствует НЕПОБЕДИМАЯ ЛЕНИНСКАЯ ПАРТИЯ!

Да здравствует великий вождь мировой пролетарской революции товарищ СТАЛИН!

Дени. Долгоруков.

CHAPTER 4

'THE COLLECTIVE WILL'

Lenin's death in 1922 removed the one remaining obstacle to Stalin's seizing supreme power. He would hold on to it tightly – and wield it without mercy.

B y his loyalty, his energy, his willingness to work and above all, perhaps, by his ruthless efficiency, Stalin had secured himself a place at the top of the Soviet hierarchy. He retained it now, despite his humiliation over Poland. But the embarrassment rankled even so.

Opposite: 'Stalin Leads Us to Victory'. With Lenin stowed safely in his mausoleum, 1930s propagandists could show him indicating their General Secretary as his chosen heir.

So did the unpalatable fact that, when the critical moment came, he and Trotsky in some crucial way weren't quite equals. He had shown himself an accomplished general – but it was Trotsky who had been fêted by the people, by Lenin and by his own troops. Stalin was quite clearly formidably intelligent, a skilled dialectician and an accomplished writer, but it was Trotsky whose intellectual credentials were acclaimed. Since boyhood, Soso had shown immense charisma and compelling charm, yet it was Trotsky's glamour that had

the comrades cheering and the women swooning.

Stalin for his part was anything but enamoured. For now, though, he had to keep his resentments to himself. Not least because relations with Lenin were sometimes chilly too. While Stalin's Polish Problem with the Soviet leader had been quickly forgotten, there had been other disagreements that weren't so easily resolved. That he remained in such a senior position despite these differences suggests how valuable his contribution to the state could be.

UN-COMRADELY COMMENTS

His loyalty, cunning and commitment may have made Stalin the ideal comrade, but there's no suggestion that Lenin ever saw him as a friend. On the contrary, he found fault with him, remarking – quite unjustly – on his lack of intelligence and his boorish self-presentation, and the uncouth way he chewed his pipe.

It's difficult to avoid the dark suspicion that world Communism's most celebrated leader may have been guilty of a certain measure of unbecoming snobbery in these judgements. Was Lenin more comfortable with supporters like Alexander Troyanovsky and Elena Rozbirovich? It gets worse, perhaps: his references to certain (unspecified) 'Asiatic' aspects of the Georgian's character imply that this class condescension came with a dash of racism too.

That Lenin wouldn't have openly avowed such views – or even, arguably, consciously acknowledged them – would seem to go without saying. They surely contributed to his ultimate underestimation of the man and his failure to take precautions against his succession. From Stalin's perspective, perhaps, there would seem to be a certain rough justice in that fact, but it was to come at the expense of Soviet citizens in their millions.

NEW ECONOMIC COMPROMISES

The Soviet Union has been condemned for its wholesale suppression of free speech and democracy, but within its governing elite disagreements flourished. Lenin learned all too quickly that, although politics might necessarily be 'the art of the possible', there were always those ready to carp at any compromise.

By the early 1920s, the Soviet Union was utterly beleaguered, beset by internal and external enemies alike. As if the disruption of World War I hadn't been bad enough, rather than recovering, Russia had segued into half a decade of unrest and outright civil war. That the revolutionaries had done much to create this chaos themselves might seem like so much rough justice to their critics, but it didn't alter the fact that the country was in dire straits and its economy in shreds.

Hence Lenin's decision to relax the restrictions he himself and his Bolshevik comrades had imposed on private ownership and enterprise in the country. The New Economic Policy (NEP) was nothing less than a spectacular climb-down; only the unquestioning cooperation of a Party-administered press kept the government from utter ignominy. Inside the Party's upper echelons, though, the criticism came thick and fast, led by Leon Trotsky, acknowledged

leader of the Left. They were right, of course, this was a betrayal of the revolution – though they had nothing much constructive to say about what Lenin *should* have done to avoid what he himself viewed as a necessary evil.

Stalin remained a loyal lieutenant – though it seems likely that he was sincere in this. On all but personal issues, he was a pragmatist. Later, for his own ends, he would excoriate the NEP in retrospect,

Above: Stalin had enormous admiration for American industrial know-how. These US tractors are on a Ukrainian collective farm.

Opposite: In Vasiliev's painting, a thoughtful Lenin is seen listening attentively to Stalin.

coolly laying the blame for the whole thing at Trotsky's door. Arguably, in fact, the NEP did what was asked of it, returning Russia to a more even economic keel. That said, its woolly liberalism wasn't what the Bolsheviks had stormed the Winter Palace for. It was always going to be replaced once its work was done.

A HARSH HOMECOMING

Stalin was subsequently to be criticized for building up Lenin's patriotic aura to all but religious levels, creating a 'cult' around the leader once he'd died. While Lenin was alive, however, Stalin showed him no such deference, being open (openly angry, sometimes) in his disagreement.

One of these disagreements was over the leadership's decision to agree to Georgian autonomy under the Treaty of Moscow (1920). It was autonomy of only a relatively limited sort. Having had its own revolution in Russia's slipstream, Georgia had been its own republic since 1917, ruled by a Menshevik-dominated government that would have seemed un-socialist only to the strictest Bolshevik.

But Stalin was that Bolshevik. And, of course, he was a Georgian by background and by birth – a proud and patriotic one, in many ways. As firmly as he had always believed that the

nations should have to fall into line with the Soviet government's decrees in every meaningful respect, he had never lost his feeling that their identities still mattered in some abstract way. And, just as Shakespeare's Henry V of England was to say that he loved France 'so well that I will not part with a village of it', Stalin loved his native Georgia

Below: Stalin's already complicated feelings about his Georgian homeland were confused still further by the courageous resistance of nationalist fighters.

too much to see it have its freedom.

At some political risk and personal cost, then, he argued with Lenin persistently, finally persuading him to agree to let him lead an invasion force into the country. In doing so, he was flying in the face of Trotsky's often-stated conviction that any such intervention was premature (in any other circumstance, indeed, it's hard to imagine Stalin disagreeing) and getting Lenin to perform a potentially embarrassing about-turn.

The invasion was launched in February 1921, and was ferociously resisted by the Georgians. Stalin had spent no time in his native country for years now and its Communists didn't see him as their comrade. Most were Mensheviks by conviction, not just by opportunism or happenstance. So while, for form's sake, the fiction was observed that the Red Army was intervening in answer to requests from Georgia's Bolsheviks, who'd staged an uprising, no one was really fooled.

AN ANTI-IMPERIALIST EMPIRE
This was a war of conquest, crudely conducted, with

Above: The 11th Red Army (Russian Republic) marches in triumph in Tbilisi, Georgia, 25 February 1921.

casualties in their thousands on both sides. Anything up to 5000 Georgian civilians may have been killed and the Russian victors embarked upon an unfraternal spree of violence and looting. By the end of February, however, Tbilisi had fallen to Soviet rule and by 10 March the whole country was under Bolshevik domination.

Not, however, under *Russian* domination, and

still less under any kind of *imperial* domination. Lenin's government were adamant on that point. And, it seems, completely sincere: as far as they were concerned, there was a world of difference between the liberation of Georgia's people (whether they wanted it or not) under a centrally-administered Soviet socialist government and imperial conquest as traditionally understood and practiced.

It is only fair to note that Trotsky's opposition to Stalin's invasion of Georgia – and, for that matter, the early reluctance of Lenin to approve it – seem to have sprung at least in part from certain scruples on this point. The implementation of the Communist programme under real-world conditions was inevitably throwing up challenging philosophical problems. Stalin had already found this, attempting to cope with his conviction that nations should simultaneously enjoy their ethnic identities and subsume themselves in the Soviet state.

And in fairness to Stalin we should also note that, if he invariably ended up going for the option that best suited the Soviet state, so, in the end, did Lenin and Trotsky too.

Left: Still young, but looking a little careworn now (as well he might): Stalin as General Secretary, 1922.

TOTAL DOMINATION

The reach of this new imperium was awe-inspiring – and it didn't just extend geographically beyond Russia's borders but reached inwards, into the psychological space of the country's subjects. In March 1922, Stalin was appointed General Secretary of the Communist Party – not as august a title as it was one day to become. Thanks, in fact, to Stalin himself, who took a largely procedural – even, as its name suggests, secretarial – position and slowly, determinedly fashioned it into the focal point for political power in the USSR.

Calling meetings, overseeing agendas, organizing membership lists, and administering discipline would have been petty responsibilities in any democratic party, but the Communist Party was taking over every aspect of existence in the new Soviet state. The economy, the armed forces, law and order, social policy, the family; you name it and it fell under the Party's grasp. Private life, like private property, belonged to the 'bourgeois' past.

And, in consequence, the scope for Stalin to expand his authority was just about limitless. In the years that followed, that was exactly what he did.

STROKES OF LUCK

Lenin's failing health gave Stalin's role as General Secretary a disproportionate importance from very early on. Two months into his tenure, his Party Chairman had a stroke. Lenin briefly lost the power of speech, and was partially paralysed. The need to convalesce kept

him sidelined throughout that summer and into the autumn, while Stalin set about entrenching himself at the heart of the Party and the state.

Aware that others shared his impatience at having seemingly forever to exist in Trotsky's shadow, he formed alliances with leading Bolsheviks like Grigory Zinoviev and Lev Kamenev. The latter was Trotsky's brother-in-law, though this only seems to have made his resentment worse (Stalin would quickly come to suspect Kamenev of resentment

towards him too). Both men would eventually fall victim to their sometime ally in the Great Terror of the 1930s, but for the moment their alliance seemed advantageous to all three.

Hardly had he been back at work a month than Lenin had a second stroke. A further period of recovery followed during which Stalin – as part of a triumvirate with Kamenev and Zinoviev – increased their political power still further. An unlikely Florence Nightingale he may have been, but Stalin visited

Above: Stalin with leading allies; (left to right): Alexei Rykov, Lev Kamenev and Grigory Zinoviev.

Lenin assiduously – making himself the single conduit for information and for orders back and forth. Lenin doesn't seem to have been under too many illusions about Stalin's motives, or to have been too grateful for his constant 'care'. He was powerless to take action, though, and had been comprehensively

CHARACTER REFERENCE

Many as they undoubtedly were, Stalin's faults never did include obsequiousness. As hard as he may have worked to make himself indispensable to his leader Lenin in his lifetime (and, of course, to sanctify his memory thereafter), he never shrank from challenging him – indeed, they often clashed.

More frequently, in truth, than Lenin could really be comfortable with. Little as he would have liked the idea that he was prone to the common human frailty of being unable to brook criticism, it's clear that his General Secretary's lack of deference got on his nerves. The more so, naturally enough (though, again, he wouldn't have wanted to acknowledge this human weakness), when he felt compromised by his continuing ill health. We have to bear these things in mind when we consider the (in)famous testimonial to his comrade that Lenin left in the 'Testament' on the Party's future he wrote while recovering from his second stroke, in December 1922:

Stalin is too crude, and this defect which is entirely acceptable in our milieu and in relationships among us as Communists, becomes unacceptable in the position of General Secretary. I therefore

propose to comrades that they should devise a means of removing him from this job and should appoint to this job someone else who is distinguished from comrade Stalin in all other respects only by the single superior aspect that he should be more tolerant, more polite and more attentive towards comrades, less capricious, etc...

It's tempting (many *have* been tempted) to imagine that with this talk of tolerance and politeness the great leader was having some sort of 'deathbed conversion' to liberalism – some dread forebodings, even, of the cruel tyranny to come. The reality would appear to be simpler – cruder, even. Lenin felt personally affronted by Stalin's abrasive style and felt that Party matters needed softer, more emollient handling; we've no reason to believe he thought the country did.

outmanoeuvred at the eleventh hour by the man he'd so underestimated. By the time he was forced into retirement by his third stroke, in March 1923, Stalin had all but assured himself of the succession.

HIGH PRIEST

Lenin's death in January 1924 had little impact on a Party and a state that had for some time been getting by without him, under the careful stewardship of Stalin. It fell to Stalin to organize his Chairman's funeral, and he did so with the utmost care, creating what is generally seen as having been a cult of adoration round the late leader's memory. It's become a cliché that in the Soviet Union Marxist materialism took on a religious aura. This quasi-ecclesiastical characterization of what happened would have been insulting to Lenin had he known. His widow, Nadezhda Krupskaya (1869–1939) *was* insulted.

Even so, it is what happened. Stalin made sure of that – confident, clearly, that in doing so he was establishing a sort of apostolic succession into which he himself might step. Stalin stood beside the embalmed body as well-wishers filed past, underlining his link with Lenin and establishing his proprietorship over his memory. He made that connection permanent by having the dead man laid to rest in a gigantic tomb, outside the Kremlin walls. As he'd intended, Lenin's Mausoleum became a shrine. In the years and decades that followed, it would be a place of pilgrimage for the pious poor who in ages past might have flocked to see and touch the tomb of a saint or the scene of some sacred apparition. What had been St Petersburg or Petrograd, was renamed Leningrad, in recognition of the late-leader's heroic achievements in that city.

Stalin, as Lenin's anointed heir (the public were never privy to the dead man's reservations), was the real beneficiary of all this veneration. His cult of personality wasn't officially to be enshrined in Soviet policy until 1929. Already, though, its essentials were in place.

SACRIFICIAL LEON

Despite suspicions in some quarters (notably, those around his rival, Trotsky), there's no real evidence to suggest that Stalin had poisoned his predecessor, and any amount that Lenin had been heading steadily deathward for quite some time. His successive strokes had been a matter of record; so too had the historic stresses he'd been under as leader of the Bolsheviks through revolution, civil war and economic crisis; and the workaholic ways by which he'd handled the pressures throughout that time. Arguably, it was only surprising that he had lived so long.

Below: Stalin established proprietorship over both Lenin's body and his legacy.

If Trotsky sought a scapegoat in Stalin, the General Secretary returned the compliment, and was vastly better equipped to get his way. Nothing so crude as assassination hints – Stalin was perfectly capable of subtlety when it suited him – but he briefed against Trotsky at every opportunity, with Kamenev and Zinoviev's support. Only gently, though, noting 'errors' in his decision-making, chipping gradually away at his credibility and stature. The dashing hero of the Revolution and the Civil War was always going to find it hard to shape an equally popular peacetime persona. There was a great deal of unglamorous work to be done by Russia's leaders and, incessantly undermined by Stalin and his crowd, Trotsky struggled to maintain the kind of positive profile he had always enjoyed till now.

Like Lenin's, Trotsky's failing health was a boon to his Party enemies: they could carp and smear, and their insinuations went unanswered. There were real ideological differences, though they were arguably temperamental as well, Stalin's steps towards what he was by 1924 openly articulating as a doctrine of 'socialism in one country' was to some extent

Opposite: Leon and Natalya became good friends of Frida Kahlo; Trotsky was to have an affair with the famous Mexican feminist artist.

Trotsky struggled to maintain the kind of positive profile he had always enjoyed till now.

simply reflecting his native caution. Trotsky's fidelity to the idea of world revolution was admirable, and later would contribute to his iconic status in the socialist tradition, but he was also to be an icon of heroic failure. Not only did his way not prevail, it never showed the slightest sign of being likely to and, fortunately, for his

posthumous reputation, it was never to be truly tested.

There's no doubt that Stalin scapegoated Trotsky, so industriously that by 1927 he'd lost his place on the Party's Central Committee. By 1929, after continuing persecution, he was formally expelled from the Soviet Union – symbolically carrying the country's many woes with him.

MODERNIZATION MADNESS
The departure of Trotsky from the scene left Stalin free to shape the Soviet Union as he saw fit. It wasn't going to be a pretty sight. Millions were to be killed

NATIONAL INTERNATIONALISM

Strictly speaking, in Marxist-Leninist terms, the idea of 'Socialism in One Country' was oxymoronic. By its very definition, socialism sought to unite the world's working class. Loyalty to a nation was so much 'false consciousness'. What common interests could there really be between the Czar and a hungry peasant? Between England's Edward VII and an East End docker? Between Germany's Kaiser and a coal-miner in the Ruhr?

Stalin seems to have been wholehearted in his embrace of Marxist materialism, but at the same time to have been a pragmatist despite himself. His Georgian background may have helped – hard as he'd worked to suppress associated feelings in himself, and aggressively as he'd put down local patriotisms as they emerged in Russia's wider 'empire'. The reality was that, regardless of the theory, even to exist in the world as it actually was the Revolution would have to proceed with tact and caution. However inspiring the slogan, before it could think of uniting the workers of the world, Russia would have to get its own house in order.

MURDER IN MEXICO

For Trotsky and Natalia Sedova (1882–1962), his second wife, the years that followed brought an odyssey of exile, beginning with a four-year stint in Turkey. Trotsky was viewed with suspicion here, however – not least because the authorities feared trouble with the sizeable population of Russian 'Whites' who had settled in the country. In 1933, the couple were asked to leave, and settled down in France, though they were barred from Paris and asked to move on after the Franco-Soviet Treaty of 1935.

Just over a year in Norway (1935–6) followed, before, becoming a target for that country's right-wing extremists, they were again deported – this time to Mexico. They spent the next three years there, settling in the bohemian suburb of Coyoacán, writing and hanging out with international artists and intellectuals, including the famous Mexican muralist Diego Rivera (1886–1957).

Leon had an affair with Rivera's wife, the artist and feminist Frida Kahlo (1907–54),

though it seems to have been ideological differences that eventually came between the men, ending their friendship. Still a thorn in Stalin's side, Trotsky survived an assassination attempt mounted in May 1940 by a group of Soviet sympathizers, which included Rivera's fellow muralist, David Alfaro Siqueiros (1896–1974). Three months later he was attacked again, killed by a blow from an ice-axe wielded by another Mexican artist, Ramón Mercader (1913–78).

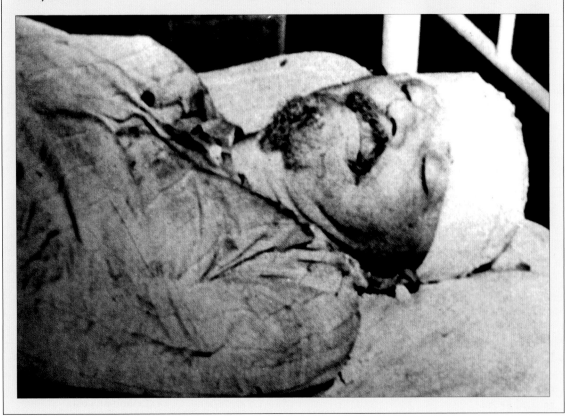

and many more imprisoned and exiled in his name and in that of the glorious future of his USSR – a future that it is very doubtful was ever satisfactorily to be secured.

Stalin doesn't seem to have been driven by the same sort of deluded visions as Hitler was. No 'Master Race'; no 'Jewish Problem'; no 'Final Solution' to it. Granted, the great socialist liberation he looked forward to looks hopelessly unrealistic in hindsight – in no small part on account of his horrific crimes. His offences, though, were to be those of excess, of rational progress pursued to breaking point and then far, far beyond; of 'common sense' carried to completely insane extremes.

The starting point for his policies of the 1930s – his view that Russia was between 50 and 100 years behind the great Western economies – may have been debatable in detail, but was hardly to have been written off as wrong. Comparisons with Britain or the United States could not, perhaps, be made as straightforwardly as Stalin sought to. In history, industrial development, demography, area, land-use patterns ... in just about every imaginable

Opposite: Ramón Mercader's blow only underlined the irrelevance of Trotsky, who had been out of the picture for several years.

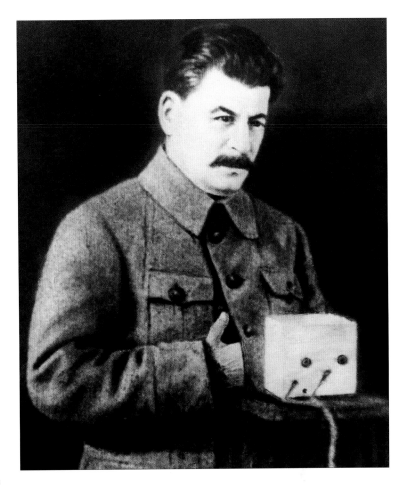

respect, they differed vastly from each other as well as from the Soviet Union. Still, though, such scruples notwithstanding, Stalin was surely right: Russia was obviously trailing behind.

More ominous was his insistence that the Soviet Union would have to close this gap within ten years or face the prospect of being completely crushed. The country *was* lagging badly and its backwardness did make it vulnerable. The idea that the difference could be clawed back

Above: Stalin takes the Oath for the Soviet Constitution in 1924. By this time he reigned supreme.

by the implementation of two 'five-year plans' may have been outrageously ambitious, but as a *target*, at least, it wasn't wholly indefensible. The element of insanity (if not of evil) crept in with Stalin's complete conviction that it could be carried out completely and to the letter – and that it had to be, regardless of the human cost.

121

COLLECTIVE RESPONSIBILITY

The First Five-Year Plan, which was to start in 1928, would address fundamental structural problems in the Soviet economy. Agriculture was to be collectivized – peasant smallholdings and family-run farms gathered into much bigger agro-industrial enterprises and owned by the state. There would of course be an ethical dividend (that profits would go to the government to be allocated to the best interest of all, rather than to the private individual).

But this was secondary to the structural benefits collectivization would bring, allowing advantage to be taken of mechanization and the economies of scale. If such reforms were replicated across the agrarian lands of the Soviet Union at large, overall output would quickly soar. Some reforms along these lines had been introduced in the aftermath of the Revolution itself, but the 'black earth' regions of the south – which should have been the Soviets' breadbasket – had not yet been brought into line on any significant scale.

Right: 'Let's Fulfil the Five-Year Plan in Four Years'. Soviet propaganda exhorted ever greater sacrifices, but did unite the people in a common purpose.

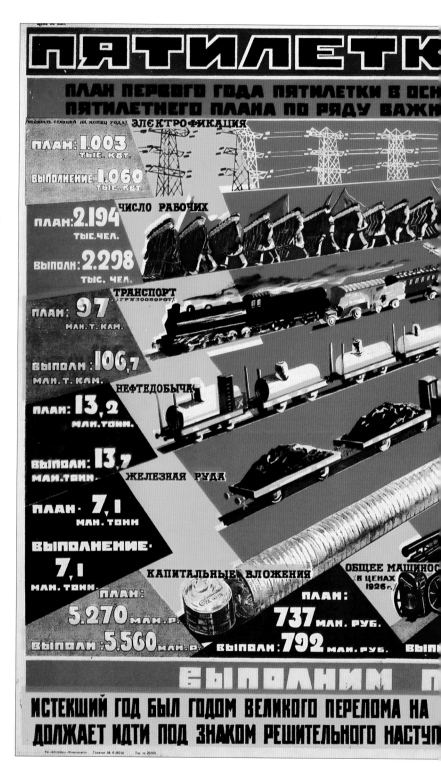

INDUSTRIAL REVOLUTION

Industry was to be reorganized along the same lines, with the same priorities in mind. The Soviet Union was to be an economic superpower. Again, small-scale plants – local factories, steelworks and specialized workshops – were to be brought together into massive state-owned units served by their own specially customized energy and transport infrastructures. As with agriculture, this kind of rationalization would enable enormous efficiencies and accelerations to be made in production and distribution.

To some extent, of course, such modernizations were already being made in the capitalist West – at the Detroit car factories of Henry Ford, most famously. But methods of mass-production were being pioneered across just about every area of industry and there were enormous productivity benefits to be made.

Backward as it had been till now, the Soviet Union was uniquely placed to make the most of these new production methods: its system of centralized planning allowed the utmost efficiencies to be made. A vast workforce could be mobilized – and, not to put too fine a point on it, moved by directive wherever it was needed, without worries about trade unions (given that they were state-run too). Officials could drive through development and construction schemes, building enormous factories, railways, roads and apartment complexes as well as throwing up steelworks and sinking mines, with no need to negotiate local planning bylaws.

It was an exhilarating vision and it really should have worked – at least, it was underpinned by an impressive coherence and consistency. The reality was that the human factor – unpredictable, often maddeningly illogical – wasn't allowed for in the conception

Opposite: A woman drives a tractor on a collective farm, apparently very pleased with the new technology, 1928.

Below: Stalin photographed with high-ranking Soviet officials in March 1929. From left to right: Vyacheslav Molotov, Anastas Mikoyan, Joseph Stalin, Grigory Petrovsky, Klimenti Voroshilov, Mikhail Kalinin, Alexander Smirnov, Tolokonzev.

of such schemes. The incentives self-employed tradesmen, small businessmen or peasant-proprietors had to maximize productivity and profits and make the whole venture as successful as possible simply weren't present for employees in these enormous state-owned enterprises. The slack had to be taken up by either idealism or fear.

WHITE SEA CANAL

Idealism worked, for a time and up to a point, but weariness very quickly begat apathy. The most willing worker loses heart when those around him or her are skiving. Fear, too, could only work so far – and was often actually counter-productive: workers met their targets by cutting corners or producing substandard goods. A culture quickly emerged of going through the motions and of keeping up appearances, of 'working to the target' – and no more.

A team tasked with building a factory for making much-needed trucks in three months flat would do what it took, and the photos in the press would be duly stunning. If short-cuts and compromises in construction or administration lowered output or lessened the quality of the vehicles produced, that really wasn't the engineers' or managers' problem.

Built between 1931 and 1933, the White Sea Canal

was designed to showcase the achievement of Stalin's First Five-Year Plan, and so it did, opening up a sheltered waterway between Archangel and the Baltic. Cutting out the

long and hazardous journey around the Kola Peninsula and the North Cape of Norway, it represented a real step-forward for bulk transport in the Arctic north.

'Represented' was the word, however: the canal was largely a matter of make-believe. And it showcased the shortcomings of the Five-Year Plan as well as its achievements. In the absence of sufficient earth-moving equipment and power-tools, workers did the job overwhelmingly with picks and shovels, which may have made a stirring sight for newsreel

Below: The White Sea Canal was built almost entirely by the unmechanized muscle power of convict labour: an inspiring effort, but a largely useless waterway.

viewers but wasn't an efficient way of executing a major modern construction project. In their haste to surpass their schedule, moreover, engineers skimped on the all-important channel depth. The result was what should have been an arterial route which was actually only capable of carrying the lightest craft – a huge, and hugely expensive, waste of time.

CRUEL COSTS

And a waste of human life. At the very least 25,000 died in the course of the waterway's construction. They could be written off, though, because the canal was built by convict labour. Of the 100,000 sent to work here in the harshest of conditions, the vast majority

had been political dissidents – a fast-growing class in Stalin's Soviet Union. What incentive did these prisoners – already at odds with the system – have to dig the deepest waterway they could? Why would their supervisors make them, knowing this might put their completion date in jeopardy?

The White Sea Canal was a special case, perhaps: those who built it were prisoners, so by definition uncommitted. The trouble was that, under Stalin, Russian society was starting to seem like a prison. Its workers felt like conscripts, at very best. Wages, hours, working conditions, safety regulations (such as they were): all were set by their employer – the state – who could accordingly get

away with liberties of which the rapacious tycoons of the West could only have dreamed.

THE GULAG

Many tens of thousands were sent to labour camps, known then and now by their collective name of 'Gulag' (an acronym of *Glavnoye Upravleniye Lagerej* – 'Main Administration of Labour Camps and Settlements'). There were hundreds of camps and penal settlements dispersed across the whole of the Soviet Union, though the majority of prisoners

Below: Over 25,000 lost their lives in the White Sea Canal's construction. Those who ended up in this field hospital were the lucky ones.

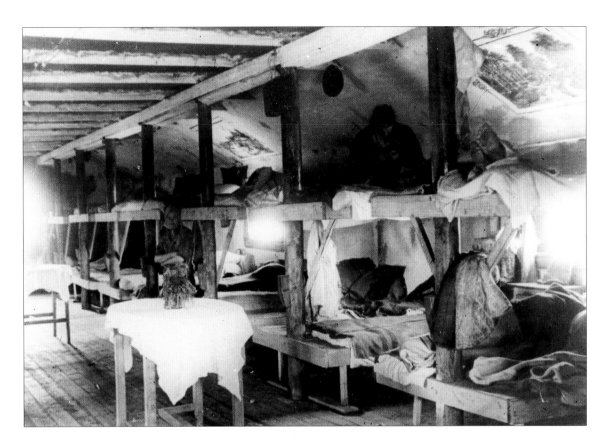

Above: Conditions in Komi's Vorkuta Gulag (seen here in the 1930s) were spartan, to say the least.

were sent to the forests and the tundras of the east and north.

Again, Stalin's share of the blame should be kept carefully in perspective. Similar camps had existed under the Czars. The Communists, in their quest for freedom, had built several score by 1921. But Stalin had certainly boosted the number of both camps and inmates. By the end of the 1920s over 100,000 prisoners were held – mostly 'politicals', though they were incarcerated alongside criminal felons so we can't be sure of their exact numbers.

In any case, the scope of 'political' offences had been widening by the year. The calculation is a crude one, but basically, in a context in which the state had taken over the supervision of just about every aspect of public and private life, any infraction could be seen as 'political' in motive. A moment's inattention at work might be seen as sabotage. As, for that matter, might a mechanical snarl-up for which the worker wasn't responsible at all. The system was sacrosanct, and if anything at all went wrong it was better that the individual be blamed than the machinery. A missing part; a mix-up in the (rapidly proliferating)

paperwork involved in any order or delivery – or, for that matter, the more personal business of daily life … Anything that might conceivably show the system – and so the state – in an unfavourable light was liable to be viewed as an anti-social act.

Hence the ever-swelling stream of men and women to the Gulag. Millions were to make the journey in the coming years. Between the harshness of

A 'HERO PROJECT'

The Five-Year Plans were practical programmes, of course, but also inspirational 'crusades', designed to rally the populace towards a common goal. Hence the effort put into designated 'hero projects' and the publicity they were given on radio and in newsreels and the printed press. Typical of these was the whole new city – or, perhaps, more accurately, a city-sized steelworks – built from scratch at Magnitogorsk, beside the Ural River, near Chelyabinsk. It was named in honour of the Magnitnaya or 'Magnetic Mountain': literally, a mountain of iron ore – and, of course, the reason for the city's siting here.

Experts were brought from America to advise Soviet engineers on how to construct a copy of Gary, Indiana in the middle of nowhere – or, next best thing, the Russian steppe. In the event, one Gary wasn't grand enough, and those involved in the construction of this 'hero project' were asked to increase the size of the steelworks and accompanying settlement by four. A quarter of a million 'special resettlers' were shipped in from far-flung parts of European Russia to work here – in winter temperatures of minus 20 and below. Their

Right: Workers at Magnitogorsk; opposite: The installations at Magnitogorsk were to dwarf the human scale.

accommodation wasn't the priority here, so thousands commuted to their gruelling shifts at the steelworks from a sprawling city of mud huts, wooden shacks and canvas tents.

That conditions for the conscripts here were just about equally inhuman whether they were at work or at 'home' hardly signifies. Though most were from peasant backgrounds, they gradually acquired the skills they'd need. They had to do it the hard way, though: many lives were lost through accidents, and countless injuries were caused.

Stalin's socialism was never about empathy, but all this indiscriminate loss of life and limb was indicative of a wastefulness of a wider and potentially more important kind. These 'hero projects' inevitably involved an overreach: in the case of Magnitogorsk, spectacular sums were squandered during the

construction phase because workers had to sit around for weeks and months on end while they waited for supplies held up at source or on the incompetently administered railway network. The same sort of inefficiencies dogged the enterprise once the works were in production as the steel city lay idle because of breakdowns in equipment or interruptions in supply.

In the end, the omelette was made: Magnitogorsk did turn out steel, and in enormous quantities – even if not quite so enormous as it might have done. If the human cost had been appalling, what was that to the ultimate goal, the greater good, to the dragging of a backward Russia into the modern age? Steel from the plant was to be vital to the Soviet Union's eventual success in seeing off the Nazis in the 'Great Patriotic War'. Vindication? Stalin certainly thought so – though many of those who toiled here might not have agreed.

the climate, the inadequacy of their food, the non-existence of decent sanitation or healthcare provision, the cruelty of guards and fellow prisoners, and the arduous – often downright dangerous – work they were forced into in mines or lumber camps, the majority were never to emerge.

'DEKULAKIZATION'

Down on the collective farm, meanwhile, things were, if anything, even worse. Again, official policy was being imposed without the slightest empathy. Families who had lived in the same houses and villages and farmed the same plots for generations were supposed to submit to being moved around like pawns. Many were killed by angry officials for refusing to leave their homes or for 'cheating' the system by slaughtering their livestock to prevent its being taken from them for the collective farms.

More important, the reforms were signally failing, and there was consequently a crying need for someone other than the state to take the blame. It couldn't be acknowledged that, as in the industrial enterprises of the day, inefficiency was endemic and the vaunted economies of scale

Right: Kulaks from Udachnoye, Donetsk, in the Ukraine, hand over their production to Stalin's state.

largely illusory. Nor was there any readiness to recognize that the lack of individual incentive encouraged apathy and idleness among the ordinary workers, that the blind imposition of norms and targets fostered a culture of corner-cutting in management and that more than fifty million hectares of land confiscated from peasant farmers for collectivization had become unproductive.

Instead, Stalin singled out the *kulaks* – peasants enjoying certain traditional rights over their own holdings who were stereotypically wealthier, so more resistant to change, than others. In actual fact, the *kulaks* generally were poor by any normal standards. Nor were the peasantry in general eager for the Bolsheviks' brave new dawn. But '*kulak*' became the catch-all term for all those difficult, curmudgeonly country-dwellers who refused to be inspired by Stalin's vision.

As such, they became the scapegoats for the massive failure of the collective system, which, rather than bumper harvests, produced widespread famine. Desperate to meet their own targets, state officials took their appointed share of what was grown regardless, leaving whole families and communities without food.

Rather than offering assistance, Moscow opted to remain in deep denial – exporting food while those who had produced it were starving. Villagers who complained or didn't cooperate with sufficient eagerness were relocated to far-off and marginal resettlement areas in western Siberia, the Urals or Kazakhstan.

The sanctity of Stalin's collectivization programme trumped any humanitarian impulse. Officials on the ground who protested the policy and its impact were shot. Anything that impeded its completion had simply to be swept aside. 'People died at work,' said Galina Gubenko, from Poltava, central Ukraine:

It didn't matter whether your body was swollen, whether you could work, whether you had eaten, whether you could – you had to go and work. Otherwise – you were the enemy of the people.

Starving people 'stealing' food they'd grown were seen as saboteurs. They were shot, or sent to the Gulag. The sentence for a single handful of grain was five years' hard labour. Thankfully perhaps, some 20 per cent of such prisoners, packed in their thousands into cattle trucks, died en route and never actually saw Siberia.

Right: Kulaks taken from their lands were forced to work in Siberian labour camps – if they were fortunate enough to survive the lengthy trip.

GENOCIDE?

'We must smash the *kulaks*, eliminate them as a class,' said Stalin. This is violently aggressive rhetoric, and it's been widely suggested that 'dekulakization' was genocidal in its intent, focusing – as it largely did – on the people of Ukraine. What they have come to call the *Holodomor* ('Terror Famine') was to take the lives of upwards of 2.5 million people – though by some, not-inherently unreasonable estimates, as many as 7.5 million. It cannot simply be dismissed as a natural disaster, given Stalin's ferocious drive in seeing the programme through – and his indifference to the consequences.

Whether it was a crime of ideological or of ethnic (so strictly 'genocidal') violence, however, is more difficult to judge. He's known to have disliked the Ukraine – though he's known to have seen that nation as a hotbed of kulak-ism too – so there's a certain circularity in the claim that this attack was genocidal.

He also identified – and severely punished – 'nationalist' elements in the Ukrainian Communist Party, though this seems (as so often with Stalin) to have been more a matter of his customary rage to close the Party's ranks. Ukrainians may, quite understandably, see this as a complacent quibble, but the symmetry between Stalin's *Holodomor* and Hitler's Holocaust is surely more apparent than truly real.

That Stalin was guilty of casual racism there's no doubt; that his contribution to the field of Soviet nationalities policy was the thought that the nationalities should shut up and submit to the greater socialist good can hardly be disputed, but any comparison with Hitler seems far-fetched. There's no sign of his ever having entertained even for an instant the sort of racial suspicions that seem to have saturated the Nazi founder's every waking thought. Still less are there any indications of his having given head-space for so much as a second to the kind of elaborate conspiracy theories that informed the *Führer's* thinking on the Jews. Does Stalin deserve our praise for managing to be a (mostly) non-racist monster? Of course not. But claims that he committed genocide would seem tendentious.

NADYA NO MORE

One casualty of the collectivization programme, it's been widely said, was Nadezhda Alliluyeva, Stalin's second wife. On the night of 9 November 1932, she shot herself. They'd rowed, rumour had it, about the effects of his policies in rural Russia and the Ukraine. He'd been the 'butcher' of his people, she maintained. By other accounts, her suicide had been prompted by Stalin's drunken flirtation with an official's younger wife at a dinner that evening – by no means an unusual occurrence, it would seem.

Either way, she was alone in her apartment, sitting on her bed, when she pulled the trigger of a little lady's gun her brother had given her as a present a few years before. Stalin being Stalin, the rumours quickly started that Nadya had been murdered, though there's no real reason to believe that this was so.

Nadya and Stalin had been together in some shape or form since the Revolution. They'd been married thirteen years – for the majority of which Nadya appears to have been unhappy, though not because of a lack of love on her part. Or on his, though he wasn't well equipped to show it. But Nadya had

Opposite: Clobbering the _kulaks_ was quite literally the policy of the Soviet state in the 1930s.

Above: Seen here with her daughter Svetlana, Nadya Alliluyeva killed herself in 1932.

baggage of her own – not least a history of what may well have been borderline personality disorder. She seems to have been as difficult a wife as he'd ever been a husband.

Clever, intellectual and passionately political, she was hardly the first 'first lady' – or the last – to find her role constricting. In 1929, she'd enrolled (with her husband's blessing) as a chemistry student at the university, but in some ways this had only added to the strain she felt. It was from her fellow-students, the story went, that she had heard whispers about the realities of what was happening in the countryside, where the collectivization programme was then going at full tilt.

We've no real way of knowing whether this was true – or if it was, how far it had contributed to her state of mind: in other circumstances she's said to have spoken up for her husband's policies. Like all of us, she had her complexities of character, as of course did Stalin, who seems to have been severely shocked, and enduringly affected, by her death.

CHAPTER 5

'LIFE HAS BECOME MORE JOYOUS'

The 1930s ushered in a heroic age for Stalin's Soviet Union – and a veritable nightmare for millions of its people.

As we've seen, the presentational aspects of the Five-Year Plans were absolutely crucial, given the need to galvanize the entire working population. Everyone in the Soviet Union, however humble their occupational status, had to feel involved in this epic and exciting collective effort. Hence the 'hero projects', publicized day in, day out, and hence the exclamatory newsreel

Opposite: Stalin, seen as the caring, thoughtful father of his nation, in an official portrait of 1933.

reports hailing record harvests or industrial production feats. Workers were quasi-canonized in the media, held up as role models to be emulated: the most famous of these was Alexei Stakhanov (1906–77).

STAKHANOV SUPERSTAR

Stakhanov was a miner in Luhansk, in eastern Ukraine; on 19 September 1935, he cut 227 tonnes of coal in a single shift just using a pneumatic drill. His heroic example inspired (or was encouraged by the authorities to inspire) a whole 'Stakhanovite' movement,

whose members strove to prove themselves worthy of Alexei's example in their daily work. It was an unabashedly upbeat, feel-good movement: commitment and hard work, the fulfilment of duty; loyalty to the state and to Stalin would bring more rewards than any ease or luxury could offer.

There's good reason to believe that the craze for record-setting ultimately only exacerbated the corner-cutting sloppiness already endemic in a system geared to meaningless measures and arbitrary targets of every kind. For all its gritty, workmanlike rhetoric, though,

WORKERS OF ART

A poet himself in a previous life, with an obviously genuine affinity for the arts, Stalin still saw their beauties as subordinate to his higher cause. Hence the crashing utilitarianism of his pronouncements on the subject – like his suggestion that writers were 'the engineers of the soul'. The novelist, poet or painter was a 'worker' and was supposed to step up alongside his or her Soviet compatriots and perform Stakhanovite labours for the greater good.

Lady Macbeth of the Mtsensk District is best known now in the wider world from its 2016 film adaptation by William Olroyd, with Florence Pugh as the poor peasant beauty trapped in an arid marriage with a much older man. In 1936, however, it was the subject of an ambitious operatic treatment by the great composer Dmitri Shostakovich (1906–75). He had paid his dues with pleasing film music and upbeat patriotic marches, but was always clearly capable of more. At this premier, however, he had to look on (white-faced, according to eyewitnesses) while General Secretary Stalin himself sat watching the opera unfold with a face like thunder – writing

up his verdict in *Pravda* under the headline 'Muddle Instead of Music'.

Shostakovich was psychologically – and creatively – poleaxed. Although the following year's Fifth Symphony (subtitled 'A Soviet Artist's Reply to Just Criticism') was acclaimed and saw him welcomed back into the official fold, we can't know if he ever shook off the crippling sense of being 'on probation'. His problems with alcoholism dated from this time. Some composers, like Sergei Prokofiev (1891–1953) worked wonders with popular genres – Prokofiev's film-scores were sensational; his 'fairytale for children', *Peter and the Wolf* (1936), remains a classic. But he too must have made creative compromises we can hardly guess at to pass muster as an appropriately 'Soviet' composer.

And he and Shostakovich were among the lucky ones. Even if they didn't end up in labour camps, creative artists in Stalin's Soviet Union were likely to exhaust their talents in dead-end projects, their lives in frustration – and all too often alcoholism and depression. In the arts as in so many other areas, it's not that Stalin's Soviet Union didn't achieve things – just that every achievement came at enormous human cost.

all its talk of toil, sweat and steel, the Soviet economic culture was to an alarming extent a thing of appearances – of smoke and mirrors, even. What really mattered was the wider sense of pulling together in a common purpose. It was at the Stakhanovites' first conference, in November 1935, that Stalin told an exhilarated audience that

Opposite: Three great Soviet composers – or cultural workers: Sergei Prokofiev, Dmitri Shostakovich and Aram Khachaturiyn.

Below: The sainted Stakhanov (left) meets senior officials.

conditions in the Soviet Union had much improved under his First Five-Year Plan and that life had become 'more joyous' during his reign.

SHOW AND TELL

To us the claim seems laughable (and not in any 'joyous' way). That Stalin was able to make it with even the least claim to conviction is an indication of the completeness of the hold he'd established over Soviet society and culture. It helped, of course, that the Stalin era had coincided with the era in which what we now call the 'mass media' had become a major factor in every area of public and private life. Not just in the Soviet Union, but all around the developed world – though, inevitably, it was to trace a different trajectory in Stalin's Russia.

The initial stimulus had been technological. The widespread availability of television still lay some years in the future, even in the West. But radio was becoming well established, even in a comparatively backward country like Russia, while cinematic newsreels allowed the visual transmission of events. (And, of course, their careful selection and interpretation: there wasn't so much as a rustling to be heard in the official media of any truth from the camps of Siberia or the collective farms of famine-hit Ukraine.)

Modern industrial printing processes permitted mass-

production of newspapers and magazines while new techniques in graphic arts fostered the design of big and striking posters. In the West, these innovations had been placed in the service of capitalism and the consumerist economy, adorning city streets with brash and gaudy billboards and lighting up the night with neon signs. The Soviet Union used them to

Above: Stalin appears in a poster entitled 'The Victory of Socialism is Guaranteed.'

proclaim the triumphant march of socialism – and of course the godlike authority and beneficence of Comrade Stalin. The year 1929 had seen the formal adoption of what the Soviets themselves called the 'Cult of Personality'. Giant billboard-portraits hung from public buildings while smaller portraits looked down proprietorially from office and from classroom walls. Newsreels and posters showed the General Secretary chatting with children, sharing jokes with soldiers and congratulating industrial and agricultural workers on surpassing their production norms. Each May Day (traditionally the workers' holiday), Stalin took the salute at the great military march-past in Red Square, Moscow, standing with supporters on the viewing platform atop

Below: Lavrentiy Beria came second only to Stalin himself in the terror he inspired.

THE PEOPLE'S POLICE

Russia had been plagued by secret police of one sort or another since the days of Ivan the Terrible in the seventeenth century. Dissidents in Czarist Russia had been persecuted by the *Okhrana*. To general relief, they had been abolished in December 1917, only to be replaced by the *Cheka*. Its first leader, Felix Dzerzhinsky (1877–1926), had made a chilling mission statement on taking office: 'We stand for organized terror,' he had said.

Towards the end of 1922, the *Cheka* had in their turn made way for the State Political Directorate (or GPU). About a year after that, the GPU had added a letter, along with a range of wider responsibilities, becoming OGPU, or the All-Union State Political Directorate. It was they who had taken Russia's scattered collection of labour and prison camps and fashioned them into a single Gulag system. They were themselves shut down in 1934, to be replaced by the NKVD: the People's Commissariat for Internal

Affairs. Confusingly, a version of this organization had been established in 1917, only to be broken up a few years later. Now, under Genrikh Yagoda (1891–1938), then from 1936 under Nikolai Yezhov (1895–1940) and then, from 1938, Lavrentiy Beria (1899–1953), the NKVD became the most brutal and oppressive secret police force Russia had yet seen.

Lenin's Mausoleum. The overall message was unmistakeable: all good things flowed from Stalin. He was the people's provider, their protector, their paternal friend. Every day, the Soviet citizen – irrespective of age or sex – saw Stalin's name or visual representation in one form or another multiple times: he was everywhere, the alpha and omega of their lives.

THE 'GREAT PURGE'

It wasn't all to be carrot, of course. Stalin's stick could administer a real sting. Upbeat propaganda was backed up by persecution and by fear. In 1934, following the assassination of the Communist Party chief for Leningrad, Sergei Kirov (1886–1934), Stalin ordered a major operation against subversive elements in society. The NKVD were given *carte blanche* to arrest, interrogate and execute at will, and weren't shy in availing themselves of these powers.

Security crackdowns were nothing new: the Czar's *Okhrana* had regularly indulged in them, and the Bolsheviks had stamped their authority on post-revolutionary Russia by launching what they called the 'Red Terror' in autumn 1918.

Right: Miniature portraits bedeck a shrine marking a mass grave of NKVD victims beside what is now an airport runway in Irkutsk.

What set Stalin's terror apart was, in the first place its sheer scale and determination and, second, and more important, the insane paranoia into which it spiralled.

Between 1936 and 1938, anything up to a million people may have died while a great many more were sent to the Gulag or into exile. They included lifelong Communists and even old friends of Stalin himself. The atmosphere of apprehension was heightened by the secrecy with which agents of the NKVD would swoop in the middle of the night to whisk men and women away for interrogation. And, of course, for torture – and, in most cases, summary

Above: Nikolai Bukharin, 1935.

Bottom: Stalin poses with (left to right) comrades Kaganovich, Postyshev and Voroshilov in 1934.

execution, after which their bodies would be tossed into mass graves.

Suspicion spread with dizzying speed, and begat suspicion upon suspicion. Victims under torture named friends and comrades, desperate for the pain to stop. They in their turn would be picked up, brought in for 'questioning', and name their contacts, the web of cruelty constantly expanding. Officials, journalists, lowly Party members, ordinary men and women lived in constant fear that an untoward comment might see them damned. Did this phrase suggest a sympathy for the ideas of Leon Trotsky (still a major bugbear)? Did that expression imply an allegiance to

Nikolai Bukharin (1888–1938)? A vocal supporter of the New Economic Policy in the early days and a continuing critic of Stalin's policies since, Bukharin had become another ideological bogeyman. He was soon to pay for his political waywardness with his life.

COMPETITIVE KILLING

The obvious way for an official to demonstrate his loyalty was of course to take the initiative in rooting out 'enemies of the people' on the state's behalf. How many innocent men and women ended up being killed to persuade the higher-ups of another's loyalty we've no way of knowing – but it underlines the utter futility of the Purge. Like everything else in Stalin's Soviet Union, like industrial and agricultural production, it became a numbers game, with officials vying to meet implicit 'norms' and targets. Or, if possible, surpass them, giving rise to a grim sort of Stakhanovite repression. Hence, presumably, the pride with which the Party Secretary in Kharkov, in the Ukraine, Pavel Postyshev (1888–1937), informed Stalin that he'd expelled over 100,000 members, sending the vast majority to the firing squad.

AIRBRUSHED OUT

The Great Purge took photographic form in the alteration of images – sometimes well-known ones – to save embarrassment. Stalin certainly couldn't afford to be seen sharing a joke with Trotsky; nor could an out-of favour Kamenev be allowed the honour of being shown taking a salute – or simply chatting – with Comrade Lenin. As the rate of the persecution accelerated and its unpredictability increased, censors struggled to keep up with the comings and goings in Stalin's circle. Ultimately, the fact that the Purge had even taken place was airbrushed out. Literally in the case of NKVD chief Nikolai Yezhov (see below), who was removed from photographs in which he'd previously appeared, after his execution in 1940; more figuratively in the official chronicles of the time. These doctored photos are significant chiefly as intriguing emblems of a much wider approach, one in which the rewriting of history became routine. One, indeed, which sought to construct a whole historiographical and journalistic discipline around the greatness and beneficence of Joseph Stalin and his Party.

Nikita Khrushchev, Stalin's eventual successor as General Secretary of the Communist Party is now remembered as a moderate – a humanitarian even, such was his assiduity in dismantling the Stalinist legacy. In the 1930s, though, as the Party's chief in Moscow, he was so eager to please that he contrived to find no fewer than 40,000 urban 'kulaks' – 8000 of whom were sent to the firing squad.

Below: Grigory Zinoviev looks very much the worse for wear after his arrest in 1936.

SHOW-TRIALS

In important ways, as we've already seen, Stalin was as much an impresario as a statesman, his reign a non-stop 'performance' of staged prosperity, political harmony and social order. Any shortcomings were blamed on external foes and enemies within, whose persecution became another aspect of the 'show'. While it served the operational purposes of the NKVD to have the majority of the Purge's victims 'disappeared' discreetly, overnight, Stalin was never going to pass up the opportunity to make

propaganda capital: hence the Moscow Trials of 1936–8.

A series of defendants were paraded publicly before the courts, many of them longstanding (and seemingly loyal) Party members. Some had till recently been held up as heroes; several – like Zinoviev and Kamenev – had been among Stalin's closest allies at one time. (One good reason, it's been suggested, for Stalin's desire to see them disposed of now – though it's hard to see them seriously damaging him with any 'dirt' dished up from the 1920s.)

The truly shocking thing about these 'show trials' was the

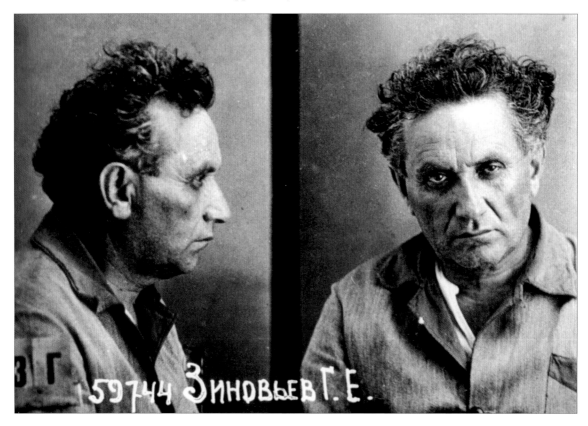

readiness of those arraigned to admit – spontaneously, it seemed – to the most dreadful treasons. Long after these confessions had been entirely discredited, they were held up as examples of the power of modern 'brainwashing' techniques – though this seems to have been just another way in which the great dictator got inside the West's Cold War head. Post-Soviet scholarship has swept away most of the mystery around these confessions: they were prompted by behind-the-scenes torture, and by old-fashioned blackmail – threats against the victims' families.

The mystique around the Moscow Trials isn't hard to understand, however: the sense of the Revolution 'eating itself' was quite extraordinary. The ironies were utterly compelling as well, albeit too grotesquely grim to be funny, as when Zinoviev and Kamenev's nemesis, NKVD chief Genrikh Yagoda, ended up in the dock himself. His very success in bringing those two giants to 'justice'

Right: Power in Stalin's Russia was a real wheel of fortune: Genrikh Yagoda first rose, then – quite catastrophically and permanently – fell.

MONGOLIAN MASSACRE

Recent scholarship has revised down the accepted casualty figures for Stalin's Great Purge. Talk of tens of millions dying is unwarranted. But the shock the show trials and the disappearances dealt to the political system, and the ripples these sent out more widely, meant that the scale of the terror was every bit as far-reaching as we might have thought.

In any case, the effects of the terror were unevenly dispersed – though no section of society was to escape completely. While paranoia about sabotage and subversion sowed anxiety even on the factory floor and in the fields, the urban intelligentsia was particularly badly hit. In geographical terms as well, some areas were to suffer much worse than others. Stalin's fears about the centrifugal effect of national identities saw to that.

Though technically autonomous, Mongolia was to all intents and purposes a Soviet republic at this time and it certainly saw more than its fair share of the Great Purge. Along with just about the whole of the Politburo, most of the Party's Central Committee and over 180 senior military officers were killed. Their offence, supposedly, was 'nationalism' – so it made perfect sense that those who had genuinely upheld important aspects of Mongolian national tradition would be targeted as well. Over 18,000 Buddhist lamas were killed and 700 monasteries razed so that their people should be freed from superstition.

The Buryats, who had kept up the traditional Mongol lifestyle as nomadic herdsmen and so were slow to collectivize, were also singled out for persecution.

had made him so heroic a figure in the Stalinist scheme that he started to be viewed as a potential threat. As such, he couldn't be allowed to live. He was tried in his turn and sent before the firing squad.

A PETTY PURGE

It seems hopelessly inadequate to say so, given the scale and monstrosity of Stalin's 'Great Purge', but there was clearly an aspect of 'tall poppy syndrome' there. Bukharin, before himself being arrested, tried and executed in the Purge for supposed subversion, had noted Stalin's bitter streak of spiteful competitiveness. It affronted

him, Bukharin said, that he should have to recognize even that any other man was *taller* than he was. Stalin's suspicion of men he'd raised up to exalted rank himself – the Yezhovs, the Yagodas, for example – was partly rooted in his fear of being undermined and maybe overthrown.

But his suspicion spread much wider, and ran more deep: he doesn't appear to have coped well with the possibility that there might be other objects of admiration than himself. As cunning a mechanism as the Cult of Personality may have been for securing and maintaining power, it isn't one that would have

occurred to Lenin or to Trotsky. There's no suggestion that Stalin 'believed his own publicity' in the sense that he really saw himself as the father of his country, the friend to its children or the tender to its sick, but he clearly enjoyed the adulation he received.

Conversely, at some level at least, it surely afforded him some sort of satisfaction that the Great Purge was cutting down the cream of the coming generation.

Below: Khrushchev can be seen front-left; Vyacheslav Molotov sits to Stalin's right at the Congress of Soviets, 1936.

Those who disappeared and died included those with the most enterprise and talent in the arts, in industry, in the bureaucracy and in the military.

A MOUNTING MENACE

The longer the Great Purge went on, the more pressing the question became: what would actually be left of the Soviet Union once it was done? What to begin with might have been a rhetorical enquiry quickly became a literal one as a swathe was cut through the country's ruling, administering and creative class. A 'purge' is supposed to be a purification; its justification in this case could only be the strengthening of the

State. Yet the Soviet Union was only too clearly being weakened, and at the worst possible of moments. In the West, a new and sinister threat was taking shape beside which familiar foes – like capitalist Britain and France – seemed like old friends. Hitler's Germany represented an existential threat. Not just to the Soviet Union, but to the Russian people – who, as Slavs, were viewed as being intrinsically subhuman in the pseudoscientific racial theories of the Nazis. Hitler had mapped out his plans for Russia quite clearly.

Stalin saw that the rise of Hitler – and his 'Axis' alliance with Mussolini's Fascist Italy – changed the geopolitical realities

Above: Workers and intellectuals flocked to join the International Brigades in Spain.

for all the European powers. He was arguably quicker to appreciate its implications than his opposite numbers in the West. In the early 1930s, he had his Foreign Minister Maxim Litvinov (1876–1951) make a series of overtures to the capitalist powers in hopes that they might join him in an anti-Fascist alliance. For the most part, though, they were more spooked by the present reality of Stalinist Communism than the as yet notional spectre of Nazi terror.

The crunch came for Stalin with the outbreak of the Spanish Civil War, in 1936. The Nationalist General Francisco Franco (1892–1975) had led a military uprising against a government of the democratic Left. Germany and Italy lost no time in sending men and weapons to support the Nationalists; but Britain and France, while wringing their hands about the affront to democracy (the Republican government had been freely elected), refused to involve themselves any more directly. Stalin sent aircraft, tanks, artillery, armoured cars and a range of materiel to the Republicans and helped set up the famous International Brigades.

AN UNPALATABLE PACT

Nothing if not pragmatic, Stalin concluded that it was time to cut his losses and make what accommodation he could with Hitler. It was presumably in deference to the *Führer's* sensibilities that the Jewish Litvinov was sacked and negotiations handed over to his replacement Vyacheslav Molotov (1890–1986). He emerged from talks with his German opposite number, Joachim von Ribbentrop (1893–1946), on 23 August 1939, with agreement on a Nazi–Soviet Pact.

This wasn't an alliance, by any means: there were no protestations of friendship or

For many Western Lefists, the Nazi–Soviet Pact was the final straw.

even of cooperation. All it did was commit each side to staying neutral and not taking advantage in the event of the other's being attacked by a third country. This was still a significant agreement in itself, however, and it's easy to see why Stalin would have been much criticized by historians ever since.

That the Soviet premier could point to years of effort to secure Western support against the Fascists was all very well: the agreement sealed with Hitler still seemed cynical – especially given its much-vaunted status as a 'non-aggression pact'. Scarcely had the ink dried on the document than both its signatories were undertaking acts of expansionist aggression, licensed by the treaty: in Poland, in Germany's case; in the Baltic States in Russia's.

Communist sympathizers in the West had for some years already been fighting a losing battle to maintain their dignity as defenders of a Soviet system associated in the news with show trials, famine and general repression. Up to a point such stories could be dismissed as Right-wing propaganda – and, true enough, the big press

proprietors weren't for the most part friends of even moderate reform. Despite the best efforts of Stalin's censors to tailor and restrict the news, however, and despite the best efforts of Western Leftists to deceive themselves, the shine had been gradually coming off Stalin's Russia. For many, the Nazi–Soviet Pact was the final straw.

Stalin himself was quick to put any embarrassment behind him, however. Just over a fortnight after Hitler's invasion of Poland from the west, Red Army forces attacked the country from the east. He celebrated his occupation of this new territory in the already-time-honoured Stalinist way, with a comprehensive purge. Poland's officer class was arrested almost in its entirety. So too were the majority of its police officers, civil servants and assorted teachers, lawyers and generally educated individuals. On the orders of the new NKVD chief Lavrentiy Beria, they were taken to Katyn Forest, west of Smolensk, where over 20,000 were shot and thrown into mass graves.

As much as Stalin appreciated this opportunity

Opposite: Spanish Communists line up outside their headquarters in Barcelona. George Orwell looks on from the back of the group.

STALIN AND SPAIN

'When I left Barcelona in late June, the jails were bulging,' noted the English socialist writer George Orwell (1903–50) in his memoir *Homage to Catalonia* (1938).

But … the people who are in prison now are not the Fascists but revolutionaries; they are not there because their opinions are too much to the Right, but because they are too much to the Left. And the people responsible for putting them there are … the Communists.

Orwell, who had been in Spain fighting for democracy himself, was to be one of Stalin's most eloquent critics, and this book, along with his later dystopian fable *Animal Farm* (1945), one of the classic commentaries on the evils of the dictator and of a wider Communist movement in which his personality and priorities were dominant. In Orwell's analysis, the Soviet Union was a totalitarian tyranny that feared and despised left-wing idealism every bit as deeply as Nazi Germany did. Its presence in Spain was an attempt to hijack the cause of Republicanism – and, ultimately, an attack upon the wider Left.

It's an appealing analysis because it contains a great deal of truth. Time and again during his rise to power – and in the Soviet Union he'd been building since, Stalin had shown his near-obsessive concern to impose loyalty and discipline above all things. His support to Spain had come with strings attached, and while many (maybe most) of the young men and women who had flocked from the rest of Europe and the Americas to sign up with the International Brigades weren't card-carrying Communists, the Party had kept a tight rein on their hierarchy of command.

Even so, in the view of the distinguished British historian of the Spanish Civil War, Paul Preston, Orwell's denunciation overstates things a bit – though he acknowledges a considerable degree of socialism-in-one-country cynicism on Stalin's part. Preston agrees that Stalin didn't want the Spanish Left to win the war outright; rather than hoping to see it defeated, though, he wanted to see a more or less indefinite stalemate prevailing overall. A continuing conflict would have kept Hitler bogged down in Spain and so forestalled his plans for expansionism in Central and Eastern Europe. In the event, by 1 April 1939, Franco's Nationalists had won.

> *Stalin does seem to have believed his agreement would keep his country safe from war.*

of making conquests along the Soviet Union's western borders, it seems unlikely that this could explain his agreement to the Nazi–Soviet Pact. Nor, however, does the 'no alternative' explanation quite cover the facts. Stalin may have felt backed into a corner by the failure of his overtures to the democracies; he almost certainly felt ambivalent about signing this agreement with Hitler. But he does quite genuinely seem to have believed it would keep his country safe from war.

Though the Spanish distraction was gone, a Germany locked in war with the Western Allies – as already looked inevitable – surely wouldn't want to open up a second war along a second front.

The calculation was characteristically shrewd, but too shrewd for Stalin's own good – and certainly too shrewd to be made about someone as impetuous as Adolf Hitler.

Right: The aftermath of the Nazi–Soviet agreement became horribly evident in a forest clearing in Katyn.

Сталинским духом
крепка и сильна
армия наша
и наша страна!

CHAPTER 6

'VICTORY WILL BE OURS'

The 'Great Patriotic War' almost spelled the end for Russia as a sovereign country. As it turned out it made the Soviet Union a superpower.

The element of surprise was conspicuous by its absence in Adolf Hitler's attack upon the Soviet Union. You could read all about it in *Mein Kampf* (published 1925–6). Then, if still sceptical, there was extensive documentation of an intended 'Eastern Campaign' dating all the way back to 1935. Granted, since

Opposite: Stalin showed courage as well as megalomania in making the war all about him. Here he dwarfs the tanks, the aircraft – even the Kremlin towers.

then there'd been the Nazi–Soviet Pact, but then there'd also – in the early days of June 1941 – been a build-up of men and equipment commensurate with what was to be the greatest offensive operation ever seen. Ultimately, of course, 'Barbarossa' would challenge for the title of being the greatest military mistake of the modern era; to begin with, though, that honour seemed to rest with Stalin.

Nothing, it seemed, would persuade him that the Germans were going to attack his country: certainly not the 47 separate reports received from Soviet

Intelligence in the week before the attack naming the exact date (and, in many cases, the exact hour) for the invasion. Nor, it seems, the warnings from the British and American intelligence services – or those from the Polish women who, in the days running up to the invasion, shouted out across the frontier to the sentries on the Soviet side. (Their claims were to be passed on but not believed.) No more convincing, as it turned out, however, were the 108 Nazi spies and saboteurs caught in the border zone between 1 and 10 June, who confessed in the course of interrogation; nor the

200 apprehended in the ten days to 21 June.

Many aspects of Stalin's character have been subjects for heated historiographical discussion, but his 'cunning' has never really been in doubt. Whereas the depth and originality of his political thinking have been questioned, his practical intelligence – his 'street smarts' – have invariably been revered. His 'Barbarossa moment' marks an extraordinary lapse: how did this great Machiavel become a mug?

WILFUL DENIAL

Well, partly, it would seem, because Adolf Hitler wrote to Stalin and told him not to be alarmed: these men and weapons were simply being 'parked' along his border out of reach of the RAF, while preparations were advanced for Germany's invasion of Great Britain. CIA officer-turned historian David E. Murphy unearthed these letters in the course of his research for *What Stalin Knew: The Enigma of Barbarossa* (2006). Along with much other intriguing

evidence, he shows how hard the *Führer* worked to reassure the Soviet leader. But he doesn't really account for Stalin's extraordinary – and on the face of it uncharacteristic – credulity. (So concerned does Stalin seem to have been to signal his goodwill to the Germans as they made their preparations that he even allowed them to fly over Russian territory.)

It's hard to come up with any answer but arrogance – underwritten perhaps by a desperate determination that, in the Nazi–Soviet Pact, a compromise of weakness should be seen as one of strength. One thing Stalin does seem to have shared with Hitler (though he didn't dress it up with all the German's cod-philosophical mumbo-jumbo) was a belief in the power of the will.

The sort of obduracy he showed in denial now takes a special kind of certainty and steely resolve. Stalin's had served him well in the past, of course. This time, it seems, he was adamant in his belief that the uninterrupted stream of (utterly consistent) warnings he was receiving from all quarters could only be some super-devious double-bluff on the Germans'

WONDER HOW LONG THE HONEYMOON WILL LAST?

Left: A derisive Western cartoonist celebrates the Nazi–Soviet nuptials of 1939 as a blissful marriage of true totalitarian minds.

part. And he wasn't going to let this nonsense get to him.

Not until 18 June was Stalin willing to have some aerial reconnaissance conducted. When pilots reported forces massed in enormous strength for miles and miles, he seems at last to have become concerned. Even then, though, his over-elaborate theorising seems to have continued: when Operation

Below: German troops wend their way through a village in western Russia in this oddly idyllic-looking scene from Operation 'Barbarossa'.

'Barbarossa' began, his troops were completely unprepared.

OVERWHELMED

With 4.5 million men, 600,000 vehicles (including 3500 tanks as well as armoured cars, trucks and cars) and well over half a million horses, this was indeed the greatest invasion force in history. It had to be, because it sought to storm the largest country in the world. The battle-front extended almost 3000km (1800 miles) from Finland down to Romania. Even so, it made rapid progress, knocking out Soviet air defences within a matter of hours and advancing 320km (200 miles) into Russian territory in the first week. By the end of June, well over 4000 Soviet aircraft had been destroyed and 600,000 Soviet soldiers killed, wounded or captured. Batting along at an average rate of 80km (50 miles) a day, the invaders seemed set to be in Moscow before too long.

The only fly in the ointment for the *Wehrmacht* was the rate at which their unprotected supply-lines were growing as their front advanced across Soviet territory at such speed. And this seemed an academic anxiety given the utter inability of a broken Red Army and a virtually non-existent Red Air Force to give them any real trouble in the rear. Partisans – informal militias – did what they could to harass the Germans behind the lines but, bravely as

they fought, could be no more than an irritant.

Their attentions did, however, help the Germans justify a spree of murder, rape and pillage. (Millions of civilians were killed; tens of thousands of women raped; hundreds of towns were destroyed and thousands of villages left in flames.) Not that they felt the need of any such justification: this was a race-war, against 'Asiatic' contamination

Opposite: 'Scorched earth' meant burning villages, like this one set ablaze not by the arriving Germans but by the Russians as they left.

Below: German tanks and men roll through the Baltic States as their invasion made lightning progress through the western Soviet Union.

in Eastern Europe. Just to be quite clear, though, the Nazi authorities had brought in a special 'Barbarossa Decree', assuring their officers and men that atrocities in Russia wouldn't be classed as crimes.

SCORCHED EARTH

Stalin was dazed to begin with, the man of action apparently transfixed with shock and fear and incapable, for the moment, of meaningful leadership. He at least had the presence of mind to place the blame for what had happened squarely on his senior generals at the front: Dmitry Pavlov (1897–1941) and Vladimir Klimovskikh (1885–1941). Along with most of their staff, they were called back to Moscow and sent before the firing squad. If in doubt, or difficulty, conduct a purge: the rule had done much to get Stalin's Russia into its present plight;

now, though, it was helping him get out of trouble.

Pointless deflection it may have been, but Soviet strategy could at best be only reactive now, so comprehensively had the initiative been lost. The scorched-earth policy Stalin introduced in the days following the invasion was, self-evidently, a tactic of despair. It was in any case being ignominiously upstaged, the Germans, as they advanced pell-mell, seemingly scorching earth more quickly and more thoroughly than the Soviets were managing for themselves.

It wasn't completely futile, though: whole factories and other industrial facilities were dismantled and shipped east for reconstruction; livestock and agricultural equipment were moved, and raw material dumps destroyed; locomotives and rolling stock were withdrawn and the railway network destroyed. More controversially

BREAKDOWN?

That Stalin was knocked sideways by 'Barbarossa' – and by his realization that he'd done so much to facilitate it – isn't disputed. His most loyal Kremlin comrades confirm his speechless astonishment at the news of the German invasion of his country; and there's ample testimony to the paralysis of panic that gripped the administration, at least at first.

Quite how long this semi-stupor lasted or how close Stalin came to the 'breakdown' some have claimed is a different question, though. The extent of his collapse is easily exaggerated. In particular because, despite the importance to him of communication and the 'Cult of Personality', he himself was always more comfortable behind the scenes. While Winston Churchill loved to lead the British by oration (and did so to inspirational effect) and Franklin D. Roosevelt soothed the American public with his broadcast 'Fireside Chats', Stalin eschewed the limelight as far as possible.

Content to let others, like Molotov, speak for him, he quickly busied himself with the nuts and bolts of Russia's defence – in many cases literally, personally chasing factory managers for parts. Working fifteen-hour days and more, he liaised tirelessly with military commanders, political commissars and local officials to ensure that hopes for Soviet survival remained alive.

LOOSE ENDS

Since the annexations of
1939, the NKVD had busily
been rounding up potential
opponents in eastern Poland,
Belarus and the Baltic States.
Many thousands had been
held in eastern Poland and
the Baltic States. Now,
however, caught out by the
abruptness and the speed of
the German advances during
Operation 'Barbarossa', they
found themselves with an
encumbrance on their hands.

Stalinism had certain
priorities. Just because the
very future of the Soviet
Union was in grave doubt
didn't mean that the business
of repression could be
abandoned. Just because
the Nazi war machine was
cutting a gory swathe across
Russian territory with
Moscow, Leningrad, Kiev
and other great cities in their
sights didn't mean that liberal
or nationalist prisoners could
be allowed to live.

Beria's men took great
trouble to make sure that
they were not. Altogether, it
is believed, anything up to
100,000 political prisoners
were summarily executed
by the Soviet secret police
as the Red Army retreated
during the summer and
autumn of 1941.

– but typically for Stalin – those of the local populace who couldn't easily be moved were deliberately deprived of food so that the invaders wouldn't have an effective labour force to draw on.

MOVING TARGETS

There's no obvious place in the conventional annals of warfare, but the evacuation of Soviet industry after 'Barbarossa' was an epic achievement by any standards. Strategically important enterprises in the invaders' path were taken down and shipped east to safer areas so that they wouldn't fall into German hands.

Workers toiled around the clock for days and weeks on end, often under attack from German aircraft. Dismantling gigantic structures, stripping down machinery, they ordered and packed all the parts before loading it on to trains so it could be shipped out before the advancing enemy got there.

Historian Alexander Werth has marshalled some amazing figures: At Mariupol, in southern Ukraine, a steelworks specializing in armour-plate was moved lock, stock and

Left: Bodies of the thousands of Ukrainians murdered by the retreating Soviets in Lviv, May 1941, made perfect propaganda photos for the advancing Germans.

barrel to Magnitogorsk, though there was already an enormous plant at the Urals site. Not far away at Zaporozhye, Ukraine, another steelworks was taken down in August 1941 before being shipped out (in 8000 wagonloads).

Partly, again, to Magnitogorsk; partly to Pervouralsk, a little further north – where, by late December, it was once more in production.

Stalin's propagandists didn't miss a trick: the way a whole community in Sverdlovsk (quite genuinely) turned out to help reconstruct an important factory in 14 days flat – secretaries and shop assistants pitching in with picks and shovels in temperatures way below zero – made an inspiring human-interest story in itself.

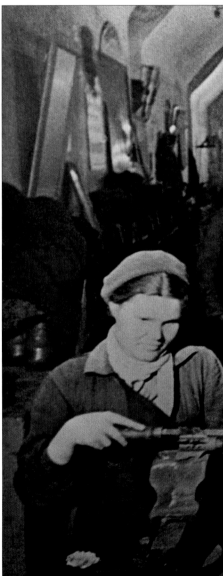

Over 100 enterprises were moved from Belarus before the Germans got there; 92 were evacuated from Leningrad. There should have been far more from there, but the Germans surrounded the city too quickly. Through October and November 1941, 498 plants were moved out of Moscow, in 71,000 wagonloads – along with over 200,000 associated workers.

Between July and November 1941, 1523 enterprises were moved in total: of these, 1360 were war plants of major size.

Opposite: This 1942 poster proclaims 'Follow this Worker's Example: Produce More for the Front'.

Below: Workers labour in an underground arms factory, Sevastopol, Crimea.

Of these, 226 were moved to the Volga region; 667 to the Urals; 244 to the west of Siberia and 78 to the east. A further 308 were taken to Kazakhstan or Central Asia, accounting for 1.5 million railway wagonloads in all.

This policy wasn't one man's achievement, clearly, but a team effort on an enormous scale. On that very account, though, it bears Stalin's stamp. The Soviet leader was effectively making a Five-Year Plan of the War effort, whipping his whole country into working for a common goal.

RUSSIA ON THE ROPES

Such measures notwithstanding, the Soviet Union was losing – and losing badly. As summer wore on, the *Wehrmacht* pushed eastward in an irresistible tide. At Uman (July–August), Smolensk (July–September) and, sweeping south, at Kiev (August–September), they won a string of decisive victories. Not just decisive, indeed, but crushing – cataclysmic, even, from the Soviet perspective: at Uman, 100,000 Russian soldiers surrendered in a single day. The indignity was unsupportable – but even so the least of Stalin's problems: the Red Army couldn't possibly sustain losses of men (and equipment) on this scale.

Deserters were already being shot by the *Politruks* or political

Left: Soviet troops were captured in huge numbers in the early weeks of Operation 'Barbarossa'.

167

commissars who, mingling with the units the rest of the time, lurked behind the lines once the fighting started, where they could spot anyone who tried to flee.

On 16 August, Stalin issued 'Order No. 270', making surrender a crime against the state. Soldiers who capitulated were in dereliction of their duty, and so in defiance of the law – the same went for the officers who 'let' them. No one believed for a moment that the punishment would end with the offenders: it was made abundantly clear that their families at home would be publicly disgraced and deprived of their normal rations and civil rights.

CHANGED WEATHER

As the autumn approached, and the Germans with it, Stalin started implementing plans for evacuating Moscow and moving his government to a stand-in capital east of the Volga at Kuibyshev (now Samara). Fortunately for him, however, the German advance was already starting to run out of momentum. Stretched far

Right: Soviet troops surrender as German forces arrive outside a burning village.

STALIN & SON

As devastated as he had been by Kato's death, Stalin never does seem to have found his way to feeling anything much in the way of paternal affection for their son. When, as a young man crossed in love, Yakov tried to shoot himself but missed his heart and only nicked his lung, Stalin was reportedly derisive: 'He can't even shoot straight!'

There was a certain depressing oedipal inevitability, then, that when Operation 'Barbarossa' began and Yakov went off to join in the defence of his homeland, he was among those captured in the early stages. Among the many thousands of those captured, of course: but the others weren't called 'Stalin' and Yakov was. The Germans certainly saw the significance of his capture, carpet-bombing the Russian lines with leaflets saying how happy their leader's son was that he'd given himself up to them.

The reality is that he seems to have been deeply depressed – even by the standards of a prisoner-of-war held in the Sachsenhausen concentration camp north of Berlin. He appears to have made attempts on his life there as well: indeed, the official German report on his death in April 1943 suggested that he'd deliberately run at a live electric fence. Recently discovered documentation suggests that in fact he committed a sort of suicide-by-guard. Walking out into a forbidden area, he was told by a camp guard to stop: instead, he kept on walking and was killed.

too thin now, so far from home, the *Wehrmacht* was feeling increasingly exposed. Although the Germans didn't put themselves to significant trouble to look after the 3 million or more Russian POWs they had by now acquired, they were a responsibility they could still have done without.

There were other, unexpected, obstacles: German intelligence had gone to considerable trouble to get hold of Soviet maps in the months and years before 'Barbarossa'. Once their units tried to use these on the (damp, muddy) ground, however, they often found themselves searching for roads that had never existed outside the wishful thinking of cartographers anxious not to disappoint their supervisors, since they were supposed to have been constructed under successive Five-Year Plans.

And, as the temperatures dropped, the weather worsened and the going became softer and more boggy, the Germans' advance further slowed. The advance of Russia's notorious 'General Winter' did not reassure them. The savagery of Russia's cold and snow had caught invaders unawares before – most notoriously Napoleon, in 1812. Like France's famous warrior-emperor, Hitler had overplayed his hand in anticipating that his forces would be safely and comfortably installed in Moscow by the autumn. For the sake of speed, his attacking force had skimped on winter clothing and snow-camouflage, but those things were going to be badly needed now.

By October, Moscow was under imminent threat of

Below: Bogged down in Russia's autumnal mud, this horse-drawn column could serve as a metaphor for the fortunes of 'Barbarossa' as a whole.

169

PRISONERS OF PROPAGANDA

The Soviet Union's attitude to the Geneva Convention (1929) had long been vague – kept so quite deliberately, academic Amnon Sella has suggested. Any incentive to make its adherence explicit ebbed away abruptly after 'Barbarossa'. For one thing, why uphold civilized standards when Germany was daily demonstrating that it felt absolutely no duty to do this on Soviet soil? Why let war criminals believe their atrocities would go unpunished?

German prisoners of the Soviets weren't to be exactly pampered; the Germans felt entitled to reciprocate, allowing Soviet prisoners to starve in squalid, disease-ridden conditions. The Russians rebuffed the overtures the Germans made through neutral Sweden to come to an understanding on this issue, making Stalin responsible for the sufferings of his captured countrymen. So the argument goes, at least, and – little as we might feel inclined to absolve German captors of their cruelty – it's impossible to deny that it has a certain logic.

A logic which, in all likelihood, Stalin himself would have acknowledged – at least privately. He didn't mind being seen as lacking in compassion. As for the prisoner question: he had to send a signal not just to the Germans but to his own troops too. As Sella points out, he wouldn't have wanted them to see capture as a welcome relief from the inferno of the front line.

In any case, he appears to have felt a more profound and personal antipathy to those who – through no fault of their own, we might feel – ended up being captured on the battlefield. Did some romantic sense of 'honour' endure from his days as a Kazbegi-reading, Koba-revering seminarian? Or – perhaps more likely – did his attitude stem from the mechanistic sense of human psychology he'd developed since, and the conclusion that any suggestion of forgiveness would

give his soldiers implicit licence to surrender? Then there is the hint of a still deeper revulsion (and here we find ourselves venturing into realms of almost Hitlerian irrationalism) at the kind of 'contamination' loyal soldiers might sustain once exposed to alien ways – whether those of the Germans or of the Western Allies. Wariness is one thing; caution (in a climate of incipient Cold War) quite natural. However, Stalin's treatment of those Soviet POWs released at the war's end was to be not just unthinkably cruel but borderline crazy.

Below: A POW camp at Potschuz, USSR. Hundreds of thousands were kept in squalid, disease-ridden conditions.

capture. It was already under round-the-clock bombardment. Refugees were fleeing the city in droves. Stalin had Beria's NKVD monitor those leaving: officials were seen as deserters and executed. As the weeks went by, however, and it became clear that the enemy advance had stalled – albeit in the outer suburbs of the city itself – the pressure gradually began to ease. Moscow was far from being safe, but it still had not succumbed. Winter was closing fast, moreover, bringing a breathing space in which defenders could regroup, and with the help of Russian industry, rearm.

THE SIEGE OF LENINGRAD

That the worst was averted for Moscow in the end has meant that history's focus has been on Leningrad – and rightly so, given the hell it was to become. Blazing their way across the western plains, the Germans had reached Russia's second city (and sometime capital) by the beginning of September: they seemed set to storm it, a prestigious 'trophy' for Hitler's *blitzkrieg* ('lightning war'). Thanks to the astounding heroism of that city's people (men, women and children) in turning out to dig defences, build barricades and generally do everything they could to slow and finally stop the enemy's advance, that opportunity had

evidently, by the middle of the month, gone by.

The people's reward for their courageous resistance was, however, to be a 28-month

siege, as the Germans camped around the city's perimeter to starve them out. A population of 3.5 million already swollen by thousands of refugees from

the surrounding area found themselves cut off. Hitler had made the calculation that the costs of storming the city were too high, so its people should simply be kept trapped while hunger did its work.

Stalin seems to have been just as cold in his calculations: having sent assistance to help

Below: Leningraders turned out in force to dig defences for their city.

prevent the initial storming of the city, he didn't do too much thereafter. Not that there was much he could have done, given the continuing crisis in Moscow and the rest of the country, but he was never one to shrink from the tough choice.

Leningrad's difficulties were exacerbated by the fact that no preparations had been made against a siege. The sheer speed of Germany's *blitzkrieg* attack had caught officials napping. Extraordinary measures had been taken by Leningrad's citizens to build defences, as we've seen – but no one had thought of laying in reserves of food.

Below: Leningrad's people endured unimaginably difficult conditions in the course of their city's siege – and got very little gratitude from their leader.

Opposite: Captured German soldiers are marched away from Leningrad, March 1944.

HUNGER AND HEROISM

Some supplies of fuel and food were brought in (at enormous risk) across the ice of Lake Lagoda, north of the city – one advantage of winter temperatures of –30°C (–22°F) or lower. As the weeks and months went by, however, and hunger took its ever greater toll, up to 5000 people a day were dying. Bombarded all the time by aircraft and artillery, survivors lived as best they could on cats and dogs, birds and rats. Anything that could be cooked up to give any type of nourishment was used: the glue from furniture and wallpaper, castor oil and even soil.

In some cases, it would appear, people ate each other: rumours of cannibalism were rife – and in the circumstances don't seem improbable. By the time the siege was lifted – after 872 excruciating days – a million Soviet soldiers had died, and half a million civilians. Ultimately, of course, this would

seem to have been a 'good news' story for the Soviets: a triumph of heroic loyalty to the country and its cause.

Stalin doesn't seem to have seen it that way, though. As St Petersburg, the sometime capital had been built specifically as an outward-looking 'window on the West', it had retained an aura of forward-looking sophistication into modern – even into Soviet – times. Its starring role in 1917 had only increased its self-importance, many in Moscow felt – and now it had become a 'hero city' through its siege. Stalin never forgave Leningrad for its glorious resistance: in the post-War period, he'd make his antagonism clear.

STRANGE BEDFELLOWS

7 December 1941 saw the Japanese attack on Pearl Harbor. Almost as surprising as the attack itself was Hitler's ensuing declaration of war against the United States. True: he was committed to this by the terms of the Axis treaty, to which Imperial Japan was a signatory. But he'd torn up his treaty with Stalin's Soviet Union without the slightest hesitation, and would have had every reason to take the same approach with this one. The result was that he was now at war with three of the world's most powerful nations.

Despite important differences, Britain and America were bound by their historical relationship, and their common commitment to the values of the capitalist free market. Neither nation could

Below: Pearl Harbor, Hawaii, could hardly have been further removed from Russia geographically, but Japan's attack shifted the whole strategic balance of the war.

REJOICING AND RESENTMENT

Britain's wartime Prime Minister Sir Winston Churchill (1874–1965) had, notoriously, greeted the October Revolution by calling for the Bolshevik infant to be 'strangled in its cradle'. But he'd also been quicker off the mark than most in recognizing the need to arm against the Nazi evil; in acknowledging the necessity for Stalin of the

Below: The 'Big Three' (left to right): Stalin, Roosevelt and Churchill at Tehran in 1943.

Ribbentrop Pact; and in speaking up for the Soviet Union after 'Barbarossa'.

Most of all, he was a realist, lightly shrugging off the charge of inconsistency: 'If Hitler invaded Hell,' he famously observed, 'I would make a favourable reference to the Devil in the House of Commons.' With his encouragement, the British media jubilantly celebrated the 'Grand Alliance', the heroic Russian people and their beloved leader – the gruff but engagingly cuddly 'Uncle Joe'.

Privately, Churchill tried to reach out to Stalin. At talks in the Kremlin in the summer of 1942, he asked him to excuse the extravagance of his earlier rhetoric about the Russian Revolution. Given the ferocity of his criticisms, this was undoubtedly a big ask. But a more diplomatic leader might have managed better than Stalin's sullen glare. Or his eventual grudging reply that it wasn't for him to forgive, but for God (the God who didn't exist, of course); and that ultimately it would be for history to judge.

feel any real kinship with the world's foremost Communist country, but the three slipped into a sort of circumstantial partnership even so.

If Churchill and Roosevelt felt embarrassment at joining forces with the Communist leader, they were far too seasoned as statesmen to let this show. As for Stalin, of course, he didn't have to worry about his press reception. In any case, he had sought to make an alliance of just this sort himself, long before the war broke out (see Chapter 5). With war now looming, he tried one last time, on 15 August 1939, British documents released much later show (*Daily Telegraph*, 18 October 2008). Only then, a few days later – again rejected and apparently despairing – had he at last agreed to the Nazi–Soviet Pact.

DELUSIONS OF GRANDEUR

It's difficult to avoid the suspicion that, in referring to their agreement as the 'Grand Alliance', all sides were trying hard to make it sound more august – and less simply

Opposite: German troops prepare for an assault at Stalingrad. The Germans became enbroiled in protracted urban warfare, which took away their advantages in superior tactics and organization.

opportunistic – than it was. Whatever their reservations about each other, though, the 'Big Three' all had every reason to want to make the alliance work, bound as they were by a shared fear of and contempt for the Nazi menace.

That said, the amount the Western Allies could actually do to help Stalin's Soviet forces was extremely limited at this particular stage. A late stage, that is, for the British – already overtaxed by two years of fighting, much of it against severe odds; an early one for the Americans, who hadn't long been in the war. Given their size and economic power, their military might was potentially enormous. As yet, though, they were still gearing up to defend themselves against the Japanese; they were nowhere near intervening meaningfully in Europe.

Much of Stalin's energy from this point was invested in the effort to make his allies commit to that 'second front' that would take a little of the pressure off the Red Army. The ramping up of the Allied offensive in North Africa from the end of 1942 gave them approximately a half-front's worth of relief, but no more than that.

Stalin badgered Churchill and Roosevelt to mount a more direct assault across the Mediterranean into southern Europe or over the English Channel into France, but for

the moment, at least, these ideas weren't realistic.

STALIN'S CITY

The Red Army and air force didn't have the luxury of only doing what was realistic; they had to battle on against insane odds every single day. Nowhere did they have to fight more frantically than they did at Stalingrad – the former Tsaritsyn, renamed in their leader's honour in 1925.

Having come prepared for blitzkrieg, the Germans had to slug it out slowly against dogged defence.

Although the city's name does seem to have given it a certain talismanic significance in Hitler's eyes, Stalingrad hadn't originally been an important target for the Germans. The advance, in July 1942, was part of a wider thrust southeastward by the Sixth Army, 270,000-strong, under General Friedrich Paulus (1890–1957): they hoped to cut off the Azerbaijani oilfields around Baku.

As at Leningrad, however, having come prepared for *blitzkrieg*, the Germans were pulled up short and had to slug it out slowly against dogged defence. The Russian commander on the ground, Lieutenant General Vasily Chuikov (1900–82), had no answer to the power of the *Luftwaffe*, present in strength over the city. So he had his troops follow the high-risk and horrific but ultimately effective strategy of 'hugging' the enemy – staying so close they couldn't safely call in air or artillery support.

The fighting at Stalingrad was accordingly more up-close and intimate than just about anywhere else – even on the Eastern Front. Both sides were motivated more by fear than by any expectation of or desire for glory: 'surrender is forbidden,' General Paulus had told his soldiers. The Russians were as frightened of their political officers as of the Germans, knowing they would shoot them not only if they fled, but if they weren't considered to be fighting hard enough.

Men ran up to tanks and stuffed petrol bombs into their engine grilles; fought from

Above right: General Friedrich von Paulus does the unthinkable and signs the surrender at Stalingrad, February 1943.

Opposite right: Stalin, backed by Molotov, kisses the sword presented by Churchill (left) in honour of the people of Stalingrad.

flight to flight on the stairways of apartment buildings, lived like rats in ruined buildings or skulked in sewers, venturing out to engage the enemy in bleak, blast-devastated streets. It's gone down in history as a heroic episode – and rightly so – but it's hard to imagine a time when men have been so harshly tested and come through so bravely. But it was battle at its ugliest and heroism at its harshest.

The agonizing attrition was ultimately to continue for five months, but the toll it took on the Germans was to prove the greater. As winter bit and conditions worsened, the

Russians succeeded in encircling the Germans. Now the besiegers were under siege themselves.

By the beginning of February 1943, Paulus, forgetting that surrender was forbidden, had faced the inevitable and capitulated – to Hitler's apoplectic rage. His fury could make no difference, though. Stalin's city had been saved.

WAR HERO?

And Stalin's own war contribution? Utter ruthlessness. He barely visited the battle fronts – not even for the sort of stagy photo ops that might have been expected of this

propaganda-conscious leader. (Winston Churchill's many appearances of this kind may, as his critics have charged, have owed much to his own vanity, but there's no disputing their benefits for morale.)

Perhaps Stalin felt that, of all the Bolsheviks, he had least to prove in the 'man-of-action' stakes and that what mattered more was Russia's consciousness that he was on the case behind the scenes in the Kremlin. The evolution from bank-robber to bureaucrat had been long and slow, but it had by now been more or less complete.

Even as a young activist, Stalin had sensed the importance of planning and logistics; a succession of Five-Year Plans and other such targeted programmes had helped convince him of what they could achieve on the national scale. He was heroic in his way, workaholically administering Russia's way to victory – first at Stalingrad and then, thereafter, in the war.

It wasn't a heroism that paid any heed to the human dimension, though: his aloofness in office only underlined his ledger-like allocation of loss and profit, failure and success. When Russian soldiers referred to the Red Army as a 'meat-grinder', they were noting an all too genuine vacancy in their leader's moral make-up. Beyond his own

family and social circle (and even there he was strikingly egotistical), the individual doesn't seem to have existed for Joseph Stalin.

But his system worked. Soviet soldiers may have died in their hundreds of thousands at the Battle of Kursk (July–August, 1943) – so many, that some have argued it was technically a defeat. The Red Army could sustain these losses, though – at least, as a functioning military machine it could – better than the *Wehrmacht* could take its smaller hit. And so it was a victory; a decisive one that turned out to be the Germans' last offensive in the East.

PAYBACK TIME

From this point on, the Germans were on the back foot in the fighting – from very soon after they were in unabashed retreat. It was hardly to be expected that Stalin would have wished to show much mercy to the invaders, any more than his soldiers more widely would have done.

More startling was the almost animal-like revulsion he felt towards those of his citizens, till now under German rule, who now welcomed the Red Army's liberating forces. As we have seen, Stalin seems to have felt an all but visceral sense that those who had been captives had been somehow contaminated by their contact

IMAGINARY OFFENCES

Stalin had been busy on and off throughout the war pursuing more parochial campaigns against much older enemies. In Chechnya, where longstanding resentments had flared up anew in 1940, defence against the Germans offered cover for nakedly vindictive bombing raids. These in their turn provided the pretext for persecution later. Vanora Bennett, in her account of the Chechen Wars, records how, on 23 February 1944, Stalin:

…ordered Chechens and Ingushi out on to their village squares to celebrate Red Army Day – and had all 600,000 of them rounded up by soldiers and packed off in cattle trucks to exile in the Soviet interior. Those that could not be easily collected were massacred. At Khaibakh, in the mountains, 700 people were herded into a barn and burned to death.

Hundreds of thousands of prisoners froze to death before they'd even reached their places of exile in Siberia and Kazakhstan; others were worked to death over the years that followed. All this, apparently, was in punishment for the people's collaboration with a German enemy who, Bennett notes, had never so much as set foot in this part of the Caucasus.

with the enemy. This went for civilian populations as well as for prisoners of war.

Sometimes Stalin's suspicions were well-founded. Significant numbers of people in the Nazi-conquered territories did serve with the occupiers – whether under coercion or voluntarily. Others, asked to support the Soviet resistance in those areas, had refused – whether out of apathy or fear, or ideological objections.

Nationalistic loyalties antagonistic to the Soviet project were an important factor, especially in the Caucasus region. Presumably they were an important factor for the author of 'Marxism and the National Question', too.

Stalin's treatment of these minorities may not technically have been 'racist', but in marking them out as national groups for punishment, and then carrying out atrocities against those nations collectively, his conduct came very close to being genocidal.

'COLLECTIVE RESPONSIBILITY'

The Kalmyks, united not only by national identity but by Buddhist religious identity, had taken advantage of the German invasion to rise up against the Russian authorities. In many cases, that had meant enlisting with the Nazi invading force, with all that implied in terms

Below: A Kalmyk soldier carries mines to his Red Army comrades at Stalingrad.

of fighting loyal partisans and massacring Jews.

That the vast majority of the Kalmyks had remained loyal – many thousands serving bravely with the Red Army – cut no ice with Stalin. 'Collective responsibility' meant that all were to blame. At the end of 1943, the entire Kalmyk people was deported en masse to Central Asia and Siberia, and the former region of Kalmykia abolished.

The Chechens had been at odds with the Russian occupiers of the Caucasus since the nineteenth century. So too had their neighbours, the Ingush. They made the most of the Russians' adversity, but all the evidence is that they refused to cooperate with the Germans too. Despite this, Stalin had these peoples deported, largely to Uzbekistan. Or, in the case of the thousands who died in overcrowded cattle trucks in the course of their journey, *towards* Uzbekistan. Those who survived the trip too often fared little better: by the NKVD's own figures, 20 per cent of all those deported were dead within the year.

Another minority with a history of restiveness under both the Soviet system and the Czars were the Tatars of Crimea. As many as 10 per cent of them may have thrown in their lot with the Germans, whether voluntarily or not. On the strength of this collaboration, the entire population was sent into exile, scattered around the most far-flung corners of Central Asia and Siberia.

DOING DOWN THE UPRISING

In August, 1944, the Polish Resistance – seeing that the tide had turned in the Nazis' fortunes – mounted a major uprising in Warsaw. German discipline was crumbling as the Red Army approached their country's capital. It made sense

Left: Tatar troops in German uniform learn how to use a hand-held mortar. By 1943, it was estimated that up to 800,000 Soviet citizens were serving in the German Army in some capacity.

A 'HEART OF STONE'

The 'quote' that 'one death is a tragedy; a million deaths ... a statistic' isn't actually believed to have been something Stalin said. It would be a little surprising if he had. Not because he didn't assiduously avail himself of the statistical perspective's tendency to empty out the emotion (and hence to a large extent the ethical challenges) from matters of 'macro' policy, but because he'd surely have struggled to see the tragedy in any event in which he wasn't personally involved.

If we wish to see Stalin as inhuman, we're in good company. He himself had noted his lack of empathy. 'This creature softened my heart of stone,' he'd said of his first wife Kato. 'She died and with her died my last warm feelings for humanity.' By his own account, stone-heartedness had been his normal, maybe his natural, state – his softening by Kato's love no more than the briefest interruption.

Not just empathetically but even conceptually Stalin found it hard to discern the individual within the mass. Time and again, we find his thinking being shaped by that. Often, of course, it was convenient for him to miss this distinction. But his generalizing tendencies still seem striking. His rage against the *kulaks* was to be echoed in his across-the-board denunciations of entire ethnic groups, like the German-descended Ukrainians brought to his attention in 1944, as the Nazi invaders were being beaten back from that territory. It seemed self-evident, it was suggested (though the evidence was scanty), that this group would have collaborated with the enemy under occupation. Stalin's response was simple, and made no exceptions. 'Arrest them all and keep them in a special

Above: As Russian as the Kremlin. Stalin, as imagined by artist Alexander Gerasimov (1881–1963), 1944.

camp under special observation, and make them work,' he told Lavrentiy Beria. Other populations newly liberated from Nazi occupation were also to be lumped together in the same way, the great collectivizer collectivizing guilt.

for the Poles to help prepare the way. They reckoned without Stalin's callous calculation – or the hostility of the leader whose last significant intervention in Poland's affairs had been his authorship of the atrocity at Katyn (see Chapter 5) five years before.

It should be said in fairness that Stalin was right in his suspicion that the rising's

Below: Hung out to dry by a vindictive Stalin, Polish fighters are forced to surrender to the Germans after the failure of the Warsaw Uprising.

organizers – liberals and Leftists, but certainly not Communists – were keen to pre-empt the Red Army's arrival and set up their own state, free of Soviet domination. It should also be said that any gratitude they might have felt towards their soon-to-be-liberators would have been tempered by their memories of the Nazi–Soviet Pact.

In the event, as Polish patriots took to Warsaw's streets to the number of anything up to 50,000, the Red Army was abruptly ordered to halt in its advance in the city's outer suburbs. The Germans were

free to 'restore order', which, in the 63 days of fighting they followed, they did in no uncertain terms, killing over 20,000 fighters, and perhaps as many as 200,000 civilians. Captured insurgents were sent to concentration camps, as though the Thousand-Year Reich was going to go on and on. Its surviving civilians expelled, the city of Warsaw was then systematically demolished. A fit of pique on Hitler's part, this suited Stalin, who was happy to see Poland's national heritage being erased.

Not until the middle of January 1945 did the Red Army

get the order to advance again. Insult was added to injury when the 'victorious' Germans were more or less swept aside and the Russians resumed their long march to Berlin.

RED RAPE

Soon they were advancing across German soil, preceded by an ever-growing wave of refugees: by February these numbered 8 million, it is believed. They feared Russian retribution – quite rightly: it was already under way on a horrific scale. Years of pent-up anger was being released, along with the accumulated stress and fear of one of history's most terrible campaigns. The result was a spree of destruction, looting and mass rape. Wine liberated from the cellars of the villages they passed through – before these were burned to the ground – helped to make the orgiastic party go. It was tacitly approved: 'Soviet soldier,' a propaganda poster pointed out helpfully, 'You are now on German soil. The hour of revenge has struck.'

'The Russian soldiers were raping every German female from eight to eighty,' wrote Natalya Gesse, a war correspondent with the Soviet Press. 'It was an army of rapists.' She quite clearly felt her countrymen were falling short of the high standards expected of the revolutionary. Her leader, however, took a more indulgent view. Apparently locating his empathy for the occasion, he suggested that people 'should understand it if a soldier who has crossed thousands of kilometres through blood and fire and death has fun with a woman or takes some trifle.'

Below: 'The Hour of Revenge ...' Soviet troops move in to occupy Berlin, May 1945.

187

Да здравствует
наш вождь и учитель
ВЕЛИКИЙ СТАЛИН!

CHAPTER 7

'SWEEPING FORWARD'

In the aftermath of World War II, Stalin built what amounted to an empire in Eastern Europe. It was grim, but it was an empire nonetheless.

' I can deal with Stalin. He is honest, but smart as hell,' wrote US President Harry S. Truman (1884–1972) in his diary on 17 July 1945. VE (Victory in Europe) Day had come and gone, and while VJ (Victory in Japan) Day was still almost a month away, World War II was all over bar the shouting – and the atom bomb.

Opposite: A propaganda poster from 1948 doesn't leave Stalin's status in much doubt: 'Long Live Our Leader and Teacher ...' its slogan says.

Whether democratic, diplomatic, international or local, politics is a peculiar game with its own rules. It has its own discourse, in which words take on different meanings. As Truman surely would have known, honesty is one of them, becoming as much an effect, an aura, as a quality of character. The 'honest' politician is the one who speaks bluntly and forthrightly, giving an impression of seeming straightforwardness, regardless of whether he or she is speaking truthfully. To that extent, at least, Stalin was honest. He was certainly smart. The thuggish, semi-literate

Stalin has been the creation of successive generations of post-war commentators – many of them on the disenchanted Left.

The only part of Truman's claim we might want to question now is its opening sentence: could the president – could any Western leader – 'deal with Stalin'?

CONFERENCE CARVE-UP

They had been trying to deal with him for some time now. The 'Big Three' Allied leaders – Stalin, Britain's Prime Minister Winston Churchill and the US President Franklin D. Roosevelt (1882–1945) –

Above: The victors: Churchill, Roosevelt and Stalin at Yalta, February 1945, discussing the post-war settlement in Europe.

had first come together at the Tehran Conference, in Iran (28 November–1 December, 1943). It was here that the Western leaders had at last agreed to open up a 'Second Front'. Stalingrad had been saved and the Germans thrown comprehensively into reverse at Kursk a few months later. In hindsight, we see the fighting as having passed a crucial turning-point by now. At the time, however, and from the point of view of a Soviet Union pouring men and resources into an apparently bottomless well of war, the situation was just about as desperate as it had ever been.

That it was changing swiftly is underlined by the fact that, for their next conference, 4–11 February 1945, the 'Big Three' had been able to meet on Soviet territory, at Yalta, in Crimea. And that they could take their victory as read and look ahead to the way Europe was to be governed in the post-war era. Very roughly, it was here that the post-War division of the continent into Western and Soviet blocs was agreed – though in theory, at any rate, all would be 'free'.

DEMOCRATIC DIVISIONS

The Bolsheviks had already made it clear that their understanding of democracy differed greatly from the Western world's, but Stalin did seem to have earned a little wriggle room. The Polish settlement was typical: both sides agreed, at the same time, that the Poles should be given free elections and yet that the pro-Soviet government the Russians had installed should be kept in place. In apparent evidence of his good faith, Stalin notoriously insisted that imposing Communism on Poland would be 'like putting a saddle on a cow'. Czechoslovakia, Hungary, Romania, Yugoslavia, Bulgaria, Albania and the eastern half of Germany were all to enjoy similar freedoms under Soviet protection.

When the victors came together at Potsdam, just outside Berlin (17 July–2 August 1945), the war was over. But the West was in a (very democratic) state of disarray. While Harry S. Truman's presence here was the consequence of Roosevelt's death just three months previously, Churchill had been ousted at the ballot box. He attended,

but only briefly: having been swept from office by the British electorate in the election of 5 July, he was here only as caretaker and was replaced by Labour's Clement Attlee (1883–1967) halfway through. As leader of a Communist Party that could administer its own elections in its own favour, this was an ignominy Stalin didn't have to fear.

By the time the West could get itself organized and try to bar the stable door, the horse had bolted and the saddle had been firmly placed upon the cow. A rigged plebiscite ratified Poland's Communist status the following year, while carefully organized elections placed pro-Soviet governments in power throughout the eastern zone.

COLD WAR

The dust from World War II had still been settling when Sir Winston Churchill started envisaging a Third: to that extent, Stalin's rhetoric about Western warmongers wasn't totally unfounded. That said, Churchill's aggression came from a place of real fear. 'A tide of Russian domination is sweeping forward,' he'd written in a letter to his Foreign Secretary, Anthony Eden (1897–1977), as early as April 1945:

Below: The Soviet system insisted on observing at least the forms of democracy. Here Stalin addresses an election meeting in Moscow's Bolshoi Theatre.

After it is over, the territories under Russian control will include the Baltic provinces, all of eastern Germany, all Czechoslovakia, a large part of Austria, the whole of Yugoslavia, Hungary, Romania and Bulgaria. This constitutes one of the most melancholy events in the history of Europe, and one to which there is no parallel.

Churchill actually got as far as proposing a pre-emptive invasion of Eastern Europe by the West: appropriately enough, it was codenamed Operation 'Unthinkable'. Unthinkable by name, his Western allies agreed, and utterly, impossibly unthinkable by nature. Still, they acknowledged the need for resolve in the face of the Soviet threat.

The following three-and-a-half decades were to go down in modern history as the 'Cold War', a time when the entire global geopolitical order hinged on the opposition between Capitalist West and Communist East, and when the heart of Europe was a vast armed camp, the border between the two sides a stalemated battle front.

FULTON AND THE FASCISTS

For the moment, at least, only the rhetoric escalated. On 5 March 1946, Churchill addressed the student body at Westminster College in Fulton, Missouri, USA. 'From Stettin in the Baltic to Trieste in the Adriatic, an iron curtain has descended across the continent.' Once again, he was showing his gift for encapsulating the historic moment in a memorable phrase. Stalin certainly saw the significance of his sometime ally's speech. In an interview not long after, he defended himself indignantly, accusing the British statesman of seeking to contain what he saw as the Soviet threat by setting up a motley crew of crypto-Fascists in government in Eastern Europe. 'Mr Churchill', he said sarcastically, 'wants to assure us that these gentlemen from the Fascist backyard can assure true democracy.'

Stalin's definition of 'Fascism' was a very broad one to begin with – and, of course, the addition of an only vaguely defined 'backyard' extended its scope a great deal further. Although it is true that Churchill's favoured candidates for governing Eastern Europe all shared strong anti-Soviet sentiments, they varied considerably in background and beliefs – from crusty old aristocrats like Romania's Prince Barbu Stirbey (1872–1946) and arch-royalists like Serbia's General Draza Mihailovic (1893–1946), through nationalists like Wladislaw Anders (1892–1970) to democratic socialists like Poland's Kazimierz Sosnkowski (1885–1969). The only real 'Fascist' here was the Croatian leader Ante Pavelić (1889–

Left: Churchill delivers his 'Iron Curtain' speech at Fulton, Missouri, 1946.

Opposite: In happier times (for him, at least), Ante Pavelić straight-arm salutes supporters. Stalin claimed the Croatian Fascist leader was an important Western ally.

1959), boss of the infamous *Ustaše*, mass-murderers of Jews and Leftists of all colours – and there's no real evidence that Churchill had the slightest interest in his having any say in the government of Yugoslavia.

It should be said, in justice to the Soviet leader, that he was not alone in his suspicion of the UK's motives. Rightly or wrongly, the Americans too believed they might be protecting Pavelić. More important: even if Stalin was exaggerating the ultra-conservative credentials of some of Churchill's choices, he surely did have some legitimate right, as Russian leader, to be concerned. He reminded his interviewer now that the German attack on the USSR in 1941 had been made via just these Eastern European states. It wasn't unreasonable that the Soviet Union might want governments it felt it could rely on in those countries.

INDIVIDUAL INJUSTICES

A fair point, if not one that takes even the least account of the preferences of those countries' citizens. What sort of democracy was there going to be for them? But then, was Churchill really so much more solicitous about what the Polish factory hand or the Albanian farm worker might want? There was *realpolitik* and hypocrisy on both sides.

And why would Stalin have put himself to the inconvenience of worrying about the liberties of ordinary Bulgarians or Slovaks when he had always shown himself indifferent to those of his Soviet subjects? In so far as the 'people' existed in the mass, Stalin might be seen as a 'people person' but the individual barely existed for him. Men and women's very capacity to think and feel for

Below: Russian POWs leave a liberated camp.

themselves, and consequently to develop and change their attitudes and judgements, seems to have unsettled him profoundly, shaking him at some psychological level.

Hence Stalin's paranoia towards his country's returning POWs. Over 2,750,000 of these, far from being acclaimed as heroes, or even compassionately welcomed home, were placed in so-called 'filtration camps' in eastern Germany or western Russia prior to their return. There they were closely interrogated, whereupon more than half were shipped directly on to the Gulag without ever seeing their homes or families again. Notoriously, the Western Allies were less than heroic in their conduct towards these prisoners – that they had very limited scope for action hasn't made the moral stain feel less.

FAMINE FOLLY

Western Europe was a grim place in the months that followed the end of World War II: industry, agriculture and infrastructure had been hit hard by the hostilities, whole populations had been displaced and economic austerity was the order of the day. In the Soviet Union, however, it was back to business as usual almost immediately: the whole country was plunged into a terrible famine. This deepened through 1946 into 1947, by some accounts claiming more than a million lives.

TRAITORS BETRAYED

Always a proudly independent people with a wayward attitude towards the authorities, many Cossacks had fought with the Whites back in the Civil War. Vindictive treatment by the Bolshevik authorities since had only helped keep an edge on their antipathy; many thousands of Cossacks had left the country and lived in exile. After the Germans had invaded the Soviet Union in 1941, anything up to 50,000 had actually enlisted in the Nazi cause.

There was no way this was going to end well. After the war, inevitably, Stalin demanded their return and the Western Allies felt obliged to give him what he asked for. In June 1945, captured Cossacks were loaded into trains in their tens of thousands by British and American forces in central Europe and sent back to the Soviet Union, where they could expect only death or exile.

With so many victims of Stalinism making claims on our compassion, Nazi collaborators were never going to rank too high, perhaps. But these Cossacks were repatriated with their wives and children – by any standard innocent. Even the 'guilty' men were individuals, with their own arguably mitigating cultural background and life experiences – but Stalin was incapable of reasoning of this kind.

Below: Rebellious Cossacks line up on the German side.

Although the war can hardly have helped, no agronomist seriously believes it was a major cause of a disaster that closely followed Stalin's script from 1932–3. Not just in its causes, but in the official response that, instead of easing it, only deepened its effects and created enduring social tensions. Again, the Soviet government denied what was happening and Stalin seems to have been 'in denial' about it himself.

MOTHERLAND, MOTHER CHURCH

It's easy enough to see why 'The Morning of Our Motherland' won the Stalin Prize for art in 1948. Painted by Fyodor Shurpin (1904–72), it's a work of real beauty. The clunking components of 'socialist realist' aesthetics are in place, the pylons of a high-tension powerline marching across the plain behind him, passing fields where teams of mechanized harvesters are hard at work. But there's a contemplative quality too in the way that Stalin stands, a grizzled-looking father-figure, gazing into the distance – and into a future full of promise for his people. The painting conveys a quasi-spiritual sense of reverence in a scene reminiscent of Jean-François Millet's famous work 'The Angelus' (1857).

That the 'Cult of Personality' had its religious aspects is pretty much a truism. In recent years, however, the resemblance had only grown. As pragmatic as he was ideologically fanatical, Stalin had sold the recent conflict to his citizens as a war for

Below: Shurpin's *Morning of Our Motherland*. Behind Stalin an idyllic scene of industrial and agricultural productivity proclaims the success of the Soviet state.

Russia, rather than for the Red Flag. He knew that he could rely on the mass of people rallying around the Russian cause in a way they might not round that of Bolshevism. For years in any case an advocate of 'Socialism in One Country', in 1944 he'd ditched the longstanding Soviet anthem, 'The International', in favour of a new one: 'Be Glorious, Our Free Motherland'.

Likewise, Stalin had softened his hitherto implacable hatred (and persecution) of the Russian Orthodox Church. Again, he recognized that it had a hold over many of which the Soviet leadership could only dream. He was likewise more respectful than might have been expected (at least to begin with) of the Orthodox and Catholic churches in the Iron Curtain countries, hoping to soften the impact of Soviet takeover to some extent. (It was, ironically, to be his more 'tolerant' successor, Nikita Khrushchev, who launched the next major crackdown on these churches, beginning in 1959.) Smaller by far, so much less significant demographically and politically to begin with, the various Protestant churches did not fare so well. The more evangelical, proselytizing style

to which they often tended was always calculated to worry the Communist authorities, as were the links many had with movements in the United States.

BERLIN BROUHAHA
In the summer of 1948, angered by the way he believed the Western powers were whipping up anti-Soviet feeling in

Communist East Germany, Stalin had supplies to West Berlin cut off. He had never really got used to the (admittedly anomalous) existence of this exclave of the capitalist West Germany deep in the heart of the GDR or German Democratic Republic. His Western allies had insisted on this arrangement as a concession at war's end, but it made very

Right: A refulgent sun and a palm leaf give a propaganda poster a subtly religious aura: 'Long Live the Victorious Nation! Long Live Our Dear Stalin!'

#СЛАВА НАРОДУ-ПОБЕДИТЕЛЮ!
СЛАВА РОДНОМУ СТАЛИНУ!

little strategic or logistic sense. It was connected with the West only by a narrow road and rail corridor and a comparable air corridor above.

In June 1948, objecting to West Germany's decision to introduce a reformed Deutsche Mark currency to West Berlin, the Soviets cut off the corridor at ground level. More broadly, it is believed, they hoped to make maintaining the connection with Germany's former capital such a headache that the West would think better of the whole thing and let the idea slide. On the contrary, though: the British and Americans inaugurated a massive airlift, flying supplies into the city – everything from food and vital technology to coal. An overblown response, maybe, but it made the Soviet blockade look petty, pointless – and, worst of all in the circumstances, unavailing.

Below: Civilians in West Berlin watch as the Western Allies send in supplies during the Berlin Airlift, 1948.

LOCAL DIFFICULTIES

From the West, the Eastern
Bloc looked big and monolithic,
united – albeit by force –
beneath the Man of Steel's iron
heel. Behind the Iron Curtain,
though, things weren't quite so
straightforward: disagreements
did exist, and were expressed,
at least at leadership level.
In Yugoslavia, for instance,

wartime partisan leader Josip
Broz (better known as Marshal
Tito, 1892–1980) enjoyed
enormous personal and political
prestige. Seen as the saviour
of his country, he had done it
largely without the assistance
of the Red Army: despite his
own Communist convictions,
he felt little debt to the Soviets
specifically.

Stalin, inevitably, found
this independent attitude
unsettling. Just as inevitably,
he had his agents spy on Tito
and his government and had
his client leaders in Eastern
Europe condemn Yugoslavia
for its alleged 'nationalism'.
Stalin even ordered a number of
assassination attempts: each time,

**Above: April 1945, and Marshal
Tito (seated) signs a treaty of
friendship with the Russia of
Stalin and Molotov (standing
behind him, right). Relations
with the wayward Yugoslavia
would soon be under strain.**

embarrassingly, these fell through.
Naturally enough, Tito took
exception to this treatment and
broke with the Soviet Union in
1949. Yugoslavia remained within
the Eastern Bloc – Tito wasn't
drawn to Western capitalism –
but its status was 'semi-detached'
from that time on. Even so, seen
as a whole, the Soviet system in
Eastern Europe held firm. Stalin
had made Russia a superpower.

CHAPTER 8

THE SAVAGE SAVIOUR

Stalin's political authority was unquestioned, his position in power never more assured. But his stability, his very sanity, were now unravelling.

Jews', the British journalist Jonathan Freedland has written (*Guardian*, 30 March 2018), 'have often functioned as a canary in the coalmine: when a society turns on its Jews, it is usually a sign of wider ill health.' Could what goes for societies go for Soviet dictators, too? As the 1940s approached their end, Stalin

Opposite: A pensive-looking Stalin statue stands outside his museum in Gori, where his reputation, though contentious, remains high.

seemed a political colossus, his position at the head of Soviet Communism unassailable. True, like the original classical colossus, he was to some extent a statue, as much a politically-constructed figure as a flesh-and-blood man, but he enjoyed quite awe-inspiring power and influence. The United States might have been the richer, more powerful nation (though no one in the Soviet Union would have accepted this), but its presidents were restricted in their scope for action by all sorts of democratic checks and balances. (Not least the likelihood of being voted

out if they were seen as letting their electors down – an outcome Comrade Stalin never had to fear.)

In many ways, it's fair to say, Stalin was clear-sighted both about his strengths and limitations – and about the artificiality of his persona. On one occasion, it is reported, he angrily told off his son (and Nadya's), Vasily, on hearing that he'd used his famous surname to escape a punishment. 'But I'm a Stalin too,' the youth had said. 'No you're not!' his father roared. 'You're not Stalin and I'm not Stalin.' Instead, he

pointed at his portrait on the wall, saying:

That is Stalin. Stalin is Soviet power. Stalin is what he is in the newspapers and portraits. Not you. No, not even me!

And yet, Stalin's conduct from his earliest days had never seemed like that of a truly balanced, stable individual. There were good reasons for this, rooted in his childhood. As a revolutionary, he'd been strikingly quick and ruthless in

his resort to bloodshed – there were perhaps good reasons for this too, rooted in his times. Up to a point, his very cruelty can be seen as based in a (horrifically shocking) common-sense practicality; his cynicism can seem a relief after the grandiose self-justifications of Bolshevik 'betters' like Lenin and Trotsky. But no amount of special pleading can finally account for the untrammelled violence of a reign that cannot

Above: Stalin shares a moment (or a photo-op) with his son Vasily and daughter Svetlana. He was never to be the most attentive father.

in any meaningful sense be characterized as 'sane'.

COMPARATIVE EVIL

'Godwin's Law' – that 'as an online discussion grows longer the probability of a comparison involving Hitler approaches' – is generally seen as an amusing reflection on the poverty of much Internet debate. And so it is. A little more seriously, though, it reflects as well the way how, in an age of ever more impossible moral complexity, we seek out some sort of gold standard and a fixed-point measure of right or wrong. In this regard, if in no other, it makes sense in studying Stalin to make a comparison involving Hitler. How does the General Secretary's cruelty compare with the *Führer's*?

If Hitler has become our ultimate measure of evil, our ultimate measure of his evil in its turn has been the Holocaust – with particular reference to the attempted annihilation of the Jews. And fair enough: the exemplary innocence of this group – marked out by nothing more than race – and the systematic rigour brought to bear on their destruction does seem to give this particular atrocity a certain paradigmatic status.

Stalin, we saw much earlier, didn't share Hitler's view of there being a 'Jewish Problem'. This doesn't make him a

Below: 'Stalin is what he is in the portraits.' Here the East German government gathers to celebrate his birthday, 1949.

paragon of tolerance or a model of decorum. On the contrary, testimony abounds of his making crudely anti-Semitic comments at just about every stage of his recorded life. But there's no suggestion of his ever having, as Hitler did, formed and painstakingly developed his own overarching philosophy founded in Jew-hatred.

It doesn't lessen (still less does it justify) the offence, but Stalin seems to have made the sort of anti-Semitic remarks that might have been heard at this time at any English golf-club; or among the working-class drinkers in any corner bar. (At this time? In 2018, Oklahoma State Representative Dennis Johnson was censured for accusing his opponents of attempting to 'Jew down' the costs of a public policy.)

Ugly comments and crass jibes were not the whole story with Stalin. In his official capacity as Soviet leader, he made several notable pronouncements on the evil of anti-Semitism and the comfort that (as a distraction, short-circuiting working-class anger) it ultimately gave the capitalist elite. Not that the existence of a mismatch between official language and informal exchanges is in any sense unusual, of course: talk is cheap, and hypocrisy commonplace. But in even

being aware that he should have a public 'better self' like this one, Stalin stood a million miles away from Hitler here.

PERMANENT PURGE
It's striking, though, that in his final years, Stalin's anti-Semitism became more insistent, in some ways more systematic and

Above: Stalin burnishes his democratic credentials in this poster from 1950, casting his vote for a contentious-sounding policy of 'National Happiness'.

he became more generalizing in his anti-Jewish tropes. To some extent this reflected his disappointment with the state of Israel, only recently created, but already allying itself with the United States in the deepening Cold War.

But if the geopolitical provocation was new, the language wasn't. While some Jews were accused of 'nationalism' – a modern, and specifically Soviet, term of abuse – our old friend the 'rootless cosmopolitan' also made his entrance here. The idea that, as members of a diaspora, Jews felt their first loyalty to each other, rather than to the country they lived in, found

an echo with anti-Semites everywhere. The position isn't quite as oxymoronic as it may sound: what was missing, as far as Stalin was concerned, was a primary and pre-eminent loyalty to the Soviet Union. It still did seem on the face of it, though, that, the Jews were 'suspect' both because they were their own 'nationality' and, simultaneously, because they weren't.

How far, to return to Freedland's formulation, did this heightening of prejudice on Stalin's part reflect a more general 'ill health' and a wider loss of grip?

If he had been slow to sense the wider possibilities of

anti-Semitism, Stalin had been well-equipped with one of its essentials – paranoia – from the start. Suspicion had been second nature for him, we've seen, from very early on. The impulse to purge, to root out dissent and cleanse away even the least potential for opposition, was something like a reflex for him, politically. And obviously, in its way, it had worked. For Stalin had seized and then held on to power, held on too to a

Below: A painting by Yuri Kugach (1917–2013), *The Glorification of Stalin,* shows the kind of reception the dictator received wherever he went.

ZIONIST CONSPIRACY

On 14 May 1947, Stalin's Foreign Minister Andrei Gromyko (1909–89) addressed the United Nations General Assembly, urging them to acknowledge the need for a Jewish state in Palestine. Passionately, movingly, he spoke of the 'exceptional calamities and sufferings' the Jews had endured in the recent war at the hands of the 'Hitlerites'; the description-defying tragedy they'd endured in the loss of no fewer than six million of their number and the duty of the world community to offer them the chance to have their own place of safety and build their own homeland in the Middle East.

The USSR, ironically, was the state of Israel's first diplomatic sponsor. Although the Americans were quick off the mark with their *de facto* recognition, the Russians recognized its right to be in principle and by law *de jure*. The irony, of course, was that in later times Israel would come to be seen as a staunch American ally whilst the Soviets sided with its Arab enemies. Much later, when the Soviet Union was no more, the international Left would tend to see Zionism as a 'colonialist' project – the ousting of Palestinian 'natives' by incoming, and largely European, Jews. Conversely, in these early days, the Zionist movement was largely led by socialists, their war in Palestine a liberation struggle against imperialist Britain.

It goes without saying that the Soviet Union's arguments on Israel's behalf were overwhelmingly self-interested. Superpowers' views of regional conflicts always are. In causing division in the Arab world, Israel's existence would make life difficult for the British, Stalin reasoned. He also suspected that this country of *kibbutzim* promised to be a left-leaning state and would in all probability prove a useful ally. Typically, though, that second thought was of strictly secondary importance. *Realpolitik* was always to the fore.

Below: Jerusalem's old city is a scene of violent division in this photograph of 1948.

In a Communist society, the poet is regarded as a figure central to the health of the body politic.

George Steiner (1929–) has said, 'the poet is regarded as a figure central to the health of the body politic. Such regard is cruelly manifest in the very urgency with which the heretical artist is silenced or hounded to destruction.' As we've seen, though, this contradiction was especially strong in Stalin, whose philistinism seems in some ways to have represented a psychologically complicated form of self-rejection.

Soviet Union he had successfully industrialized and then led it to victory in the War. But the *efficiency* with which it had worked was questionable. The costs of this success had been unimaginable and the life it had secured its citizens for the most part deeply grim.

Where, moreover, was it going to end? At what point would Stalin (or his people) be in a position to relax, to feel that something like a stable order had been established and some kind of settled social harmony achieved? That, it turned out, was the last thing Stalin wanted.

That the opening shots in his renewed assault on the nation's psychic equilibrium should have taken the form of hostile poetry reviews seems completely incomprehensible to the modern Western reader and says much about the Soviet Union at this time. The denunciation of new publications by the poet Anna Akhmatova (1889–1966) and the satirist Mikhail Zoschenko (1894–1958) was a clear warning to Russia's writers and artists – and hence to the Soviet Union at large. 'In a Communist society', the critic

Above: The popular Leningrad writer Mikhail Zoschenko suddenly found himself an enemy of the state.

THE LENINGRAD AFFAIR

The attack on Akhmatova and Zoschenko sent a more specific message to the city of Leningrad, with which both these writers were closely associated. Zoschenko was actually a native of the place, and Akhmatova had made her life there and become a sort of figurehead for its effervescent intellectual and artistic life.

It was to be closely followed by an attack upon the political establishment of Leningrad – riding far too high now, Stalin felt, thanks to the Siege. In 1949, the decision by Aleksei Kuznetsov (1895–50), Nikolai Voznesensky (1903–50) and other leading Leningrad officials to organize a trade fair for the city smacked too much of self-willed independence for Stalin's taste. They were accused of corruption – of using arrangements for the fair to embezzle federal funds – and of attempting to promote Leningrad as an alternative capital. (And, by extension, perhaps, of promoting a wider openness towards the outside world on the part of the Soviet Union at large, as against Stalin's ideal of 'socialism in one country'.)

Lavrentiy Beria organized the attack on the Leningrad leadership, though the direct accuser was Georgy Malenkov (1902–88). Endlessly useful (and unstintingly unscrupulous), Malenkov made himself Stalin's 'golden boy' in the post-war years. In addition to arraigning six senior officials – including Leningrad's mayor on capital treason charges (all were executed), he had some 200 other officials imprisoned or exiled for lengthy terms. And this was the tip of the iceberg. While those hundreds of men and women (as many as 2000) sent into exile for lesser periods could consider themselves comparatively lucky, their lost contributions to the life of the city couldn't readily be measured. The cream of Leningrad's writers, artists, scholars, scientists and even schoolteachers, they had been an important part of what had made the city great and it

Left: Always Stalin's loyal supporter, Aleksei Kuznetsov was one who bore the brunt when Stalin's attitude to Leningrad turned sour.

ANNA, AIRS AND GRACES

'I am not one of those who abandoned their country/To the wounds administered by the enemy ...' read the opening lines of a famous poem by Anna Akhmatova. Had they been written just a few years earlier, at the time of the Revolution, the interpretation would have been available that the 'enemy' referred to was the Germany of World War I. But this poem was composed in 1922.

Born outside Odessa, on the Black Sea coast, Akhmatova had made her life in St Petersburg from an early age. Of aristocratic background, she had lived the bohemian life in the West for some years before settling back in her home city. She could easily have emigrated after the Revolution (and does seem to have been tempted), but couldn't finally bring herself to leave.

If the sentiments hadn't been offensive enough, the way they were delivered, with all the stylish poise of the salon put-down, would surely have infuriated Stalin beyond endurance. With her well-bred beauty and flamboyant sophistication, Akhmatova embodied everything he loathed about Leningrad.

It has to have been on his authority that, in 1946, her work was condemned outright, as 'pessimistic' (a grave offence in a Soviet Union in which the poet was deemed to have a duty to be upbeat for the greater good). It was also, in the opinion of reviewers in the Party journals, deeply decadent and 'bourgeois'. Akhmatova was expelled from the Writer's Union – which meant that, officially, she couldn't work. For the next few years, she lived in penury and her son was arrested on dubious-sounding charges and sent to Siberia. After Stalin's death, she was to some extent rehabilitated, though her 'upper-class' and 'mystic' poetic styles were always going to make her position problematic.

Below: Anna Akhmatova was a highly accomplished poet.

THE PERILS OF POLINA

Polina Zhemchuzhina (1897–1970), had served at a senior level – first as Minister of Fisheries and then from 1939 in overall charge of the textiles industry. She was the Soviet Union's only female official of that rank. She was also the adored wife of Vyacheslav Molotov, who described her as not only 'beautiful and intelligent' but 'a real Bolshevik'. The complete package, as far as the Foreign Minister was concerned...

She was not so much to the General Secretary's taste, though. Stalin had long had his suspicions of Polina – or, if not of her exactly, at least of her former friendship with his late wife, Nadezhda Alliluyeva. She had been the last person to speak to Nadya before she took her life. Did Stalin wonder what compromising secrets she'd been told?

That wasn't all. Born Perl Karpovskaya (Polina is Russian for 'Pearl'), she was the daughter of a Jewish tailor and, as a fluent Yiddish-speaker, had helped interpret at meetings between her husband and Golda Meir (1898–1978). At this time, Israel's future prime minister was its first ambassador to the USSR. That Polina and Golda became good friends did not sit well with Stalin.

In 1948 Zhemchuzhina was arrested and accused of treason. Much as Molotov loved her, he knew better than to disregard

Above: Polina Zhemchuzhina was born into the wrong race at the wrong time.

the General Secretary's direct order that he divorce her – it would surely have increased her difficulties as well as his. Just to complete her humiliation, at her show trial, two male prisoners were pressured into saying that they'd had 'group sex' with her. Zhemchuzhina was convicted, sent into exile and wouldn't be allowed to see her husband again in Stalin's lifetime. After Stalin's death, she came back from Kazakhstan to be reunited with her husband and – still staunch in her Bolshevism – lived happy ever after.

was dismally diminished by their expulsion.

SEND FOR THE DOCTOR

In 1951, a Jewish doctor, Yakov Etinger (1887–1951), died in prison – very likely as a result of his harsh treatment there. His chief persecutor, the senior secret policeman Mikhail Ryumin (1913–54), insisted that Etinger had helped kill Stalin's late lieutenant Andrei Zhdanov (1896–1948) three years before.

Zhdanov's best friends (who for much of his life had included the General Secretary) had admitted that he didn't have the healthiest of lifestyles. Stalin had upbraided him ceaselessly about his alcoholism. But the thought that 'the Jews' – and, in particular, those Jews tasked with caring and curing – might actually be poisoning their most important patients (and so, metaphorically, the Soviet state) was too enticing to the anti-Semitic mind-set to be resisted.

No softie himself, Ryumin's boss, Viktor Abakumov (1908–54), was notorious for his hands-on approach to interrogation. Generally speaking, he was as anti-Semitic as the next torturer in Stalin's state. Even so, he dismissed Ryumin's allegations against Yakov Etinger as ridiculous – because, of course, they were – only to find himself denounced for (basically) not trying hard enough against the Jews.

In 1952, new evidence emerged of genuine irregularities around Zhdanov's death – though only of 'cock-up', not conspiracy. The gravity of Zhdanov's heart condition had been missed, and after his death doctors had assisted in a

Below: Andrei Zhdanov's death precipitated Stalin's paranoia against the Jews.

cover-up – though none of these practitioners had been Jews. Hence the dusting-off of the Etinger file and the relaunch of the investigation as, essentially, a bureaucratically-managed pogrom. In the best traditions of the Stalinist purge, the thirty-odd Jewish doctors arrested at the outset were tortured into implicating many more. The conspirators, it was claimed, had hoped to take advantage of their professional skills and privileged access to assassinate key figures, such as Malenkov, Moscow Party chief Nikita Khrushchev and even, it was alleged, Stalin himself. A carefully co-ordinated press campaign drove home the message that international Jewry was out to undermine the Soviet state in the most insidious way and that its citizens had to stay loyal in response.

Stalin himself, in fairness, pointed out that there was practically nothing in the way of evidence for the existence of a 'Doctors' Plot'. Being Stalin, however, his solution to this

difficulty was not to disband the investigation but to demand that his torturers up their game.

In the end, ironically, the accused were to be saved by a new – and this time real – medical emergency. Some time during the night of 1 March 1953, Stalin's staff members found him lying, alive but helpless and more or less incapable of speech, on the bedroom floor of his *dacha*, not far from Moscow. He had suffered a cerebral haemorrhage.

AN UNDIGNIFIED END

Given the general paranoia surrounding their leader, those who found him were afraid to summon help. Not so much because they really believed that a doctor might wish their master harm, but because they feared being accused of having poisoned him or of deliberately trying to create a public panic. After moving Stalin to a couch, for the first 12 hours they simply played for time.

Once Stalin's chief lieutenants had been told by the staff, they also played for time. Beria believed he might be blamed himself, accused of having Stalin poisoned. (Perhaps, some historians have suggested, because he had: Stalin is known to have turned against his Minister for Internal Affairs.) Malenkov, Khrushchev and Nikolai Bulganin (1895–1975) would have been concerned to shore up their own positions prior to the scramble for political advantage that was bound to come. The longer Stalin took to die, the better, as far as they were

Opposite: Malenkov, Beria, Bulganin and Molotov meet after Stalin's death to inaugurate what the western press would see as a Shakespearean succession struggle.

Below: Attended by officials, Stalin's coffin makes its stately way to its resting-place in Lenin's Mausoleum.

La morte di Stalin. L'angosciata veglia nella triste anticamera del Cremlino mentre il Maresciallo si spegne lentamente. Seduti in primo piano Malenkov (a sinistra) e Beria. In piedi al centro da sinistra Bulganin, Molotov, Voroscilov e Mikoyan. In secondo piano Kaganovic. (Disegno di Walter Molino)

concerned. However, it appears – in yet another example of Stalin's paradoxical personality and perverse appeal – that these cold Machiavels were also genuinely upset. Lavrentiy Beria's wife Nina (Gegechkori, 1905–91) had every reason to believe that Stalin would have had her killed with her husband – yet she wept inconsolably to hear of his impending death.

Stalin died on 5 March 1953. An autopsy revealed that he had died of a cerebral haemorrhage.

WHAT NEXT?

Stalin's death was, as the cliché has it, the end of an era. A generation of Russians literally couldn't imagine a life under any other leader. There's no reason, then, to doubt the sincerity of those who turned out to witness his state funeral in their many tens of thousands (several died – maybe more than a hundred – in the crush). 'Stockholm Syndrome', perhaps, but it was no less real for all that. Few doubted the fittingness of the embalmed corpse of the late leader being laid to rest alongside his supposed mentor in Lenin's Mausoleum.

Those who'd been closer to him in life felt a great deal more detachment in death. Beria made a bid for power – and a belated swing to liberalism. Malenkov and Khrushchev ganged up on him for his pains. After Beria's execution (shot through the forehead in the prison cell in

Below: Business as usual – in public, at least. Khrushchev and Malenkov make nice for a visit to a collective farm, June 1954.

Stalin was at very least the devil Soviet citizens knew. Vast crowds came out to mourn him – even, here, in Leningrad.

which he'd been shackled), Malenkov stepped in, only to be shouldered aside as General Secretary by Bulganin. It was, however, Nikita Khrushchev who finally emerged as Stalin's successor.

Khrushchev had been a loyal supporter of Stalin in his day, positively eager in his participation in the Great Purge in Moscow. Now, however, he condemned the late leader, denounced his Cult of Personality and set about dismantling many of the structures of his state. Stalin had been an anti-socialist aberration: he never should have a 'successor' in anything like the fullest sense. A system of 'collective leadership' was needed, Khrushchev said. No one man should be able to accumulate the kind of absolute power that Joseph Stalin had done. And so it was. The Soviet Union might still, from that point on, never have anything remotely resembling a democracy, but neither was it to have another Stalin.

If Khrushchev and his comrades had anything to do with it, there was to be no memory of Stalin. 'De-Stalinization' didn't stop at rescinding the late dictator's

Right: Lenin's Mausoleum once more: crowds file in to pay their respects after the removal of Stalin's body in 1961.

legal measures or reversing his policies. It renamed towns and institutions that had been named after him and it took down statues and other monuments. His name was discreetly dropped from the national anthem. His words and many of his actions disappeared from schoolbooks and academic studies. Symbolically, in 1961, his body was removed from its enshrined position at Lenin's side and relocated to a grave by the Kremlin wall.

Khrushchev's famous 'Secret Speech' of February 1956 was to begrudge the dictator what might have been seen as his one indisputable achievement: the victory he'd helped bring his country in World War II.

IRREPRESSIBLE

It was never going to be that easy, of course. The public discourse was all very well, but the experiences of men and women weren't to be cancelled out by the renaming of a health clinic, and their memories weren't to be deleted by a stroke of the censor's pen. And not just the negative experiences and memories. A generation had lived its whole life under Stalin – and not just in unhappiness, but in the good times too. His portrait had looked down on them in fatherly protectiveness when they'd graduated or completed their apprenticeships, fallen in love, got married, registered their newborn babies.

Nor, after so many years' 'hard sell' on Stalin's inestimable virtues, could they simply switch off their veneration for the man.

Stalin's native Georgia was particularly conflicted (this ambivalence was to be an enduring one). Their local boy had left them early and thereafter he'd done a great deal to repress their national identity. Nevertheless, he had been their local boy. Demonstrations against de-Stalinization in the Republic – flaring up around the removal of monuments and statues – led to serious outbreaks of rioting in some cases.

But Georgia's difficulties in dealing with the Stalin legacy in all its complexities were only a more concentrated version of those experienced across the Soviet Union. Stalin had made their country a hellhole, but he had also made it proud. The defining moment in the modern history of every participating

nation, World War II had loomed especially large in the USSR, where it had claimed so many millions of casualties. Whatever mistakes he may have made in the lead-up to the fighting, Stalin had been the helmsman who'd brought the country through and would always be inseparably associated with that triumph.

There we have him. Eternally, irredeemably contradictory. 'Man or monster?' The question makes no sense. That he was so obviously both and that this fact causes us to wonder what either humanity or monstrosity consist of is surely key to Stalin's continuing fascination.

Opposite and below: A woman lays flowers on his tomb on the 125th anniversary of his birth, while a Communist carries Stalin's portrait as part of the recent rehabilitation of the dictator's reputation.

Bibliography

Applebaum, Anne. *Gulag: A History of the Soviet Camps* (London: Allen Lane, 2003).

———. *Gulag Voices: An Anthology* (New Haven, CT: Yale, 2011).

———. *Iron Curtain: The Crushing of Eastern Europe, 1944–56* (London: Penguin, 2012).

Beevor, Antony. *Berlin: The Downfall, 1945* (London: Viking, 2002).

Bennett, Vanora. *Crying Wolf: The Return of War to Chechnya* (London: Picador, 1998).

Bullock, Alan. *Hitler and Stalin: Parallel Lives* (London: Collins, 1993).

Haslam, Jonathan. *Russia's Cold War* (New Haven, CT: Yale, 2011).

Khlevniuk, Oleg V. *Stalin: New Biography of a Dictator* (New Haven/London: Yale University Press, 2015).

Merridale, Catherine. *Ivan's War: Inside the Red Army, 1939–45* (London, 2005).

Murphy, David E. *What Stalin Knew: The Enigma of Barbarossa* (New Haven, CT: Yale, 2005).

Overy, Richard. *Russia's War: Blood Upon the Snow* (London: Penguin, 1997).

Preston, Paul. *The Spanish Civil War: Reaction, Revolution and Revenge* (London: HarperCollins, 2006).

Rayfield, Donald. *Stalin and his Hangmen: The Tyrant and Those who Killed for him* (New York: Random House, 2004).

Reid, Anna. *Borderland: A Journey Through the History of Ukraine* (London: Orion, 1999).

———. *Leningrad: Tragedy of a City Under Siege, 1941–44* (London: Bloomsbury, 2011).

Sebag-Montefiore, Simon. *Young Stalin* (London: Weidenfeld & Nicolson, 2007).

———. *Stalin: The Court of the Red Tsar* (London: Weidenfeld & Nicolson, 2003).

Sella, Amnon. *The Value of Human Life in Soviet Warfare* (London: Routledge, 2015).

Service, Robert. *The Penguin History of Modern Russia: From Tsarism to the Twenty-First Century* (London: Penguin, 2015).

———. *Stalin: A Biography* (London: Macmillan, 2005).

Werth, Alexander. *Russia at War, 1941–1945* (London: Carroll & Graf, 1997).

Picture Credits

Index

References to illustrations are in *italics*.

Abakumov, Viktor 211
Achinsk 90–1, *90–1*
Adelkhanov factory, Tbilisi 40, 64–5
agriculture
    collectivization 122, 125, 132–6, 137
    Kulaks 132–5, 134, 136, 148
Akhmatova, Anna 207–9, *209*
Alexander III, Czar 12
Alexandra, Empress 89
Alexei, Czarevich 89
All-Union State Political Directorate 143
Alliluyev, Sergei 57
Alliluyeva, Nadezhda (Nadya) 57, 81, 96–7, 137, *137*, 210
    death of 137
Alliluyeva, Olga 57, 96–7
Alliluyeva, Svetlana (Stalin's daughter) *137, 202*
Alvabarsk printing shop, Tbilisi 59
anti-Semitism 204–6, 211–12
Armenians 60
arts 140–1, 207–9
Azeris 60

Bailov prison, Baku *67*, 74
Baku 60, *72*, 74, 76
    Bailov prison *67*, 74
bank robbery 68–73
Battle Squads 60, 64
Batumi, Georgia 54–6, *54–5*
Bennett, Vanora 182
Beria, Lavrentiy 38, *143*, 152, 185, 208, 212, 213, 214
Beria, Nina 38, 212, 214
Berlin
    Berlin Airlift 197–8, *198*
    capture of 19, 187, *187*
Beso (Besarion Djugashvili) 32–6, 33, 38,–40, 42–3
Bloody Sunday *58*, 59
Brest-Litovsk Treaty (1918) 101, 103
Brezhnev, Leonid 28
Britain
    Berlin Airlift 198
    Churchill, Winston *177*, 177–8, *181*, 182, 189–90, *190*, 191–4
    Fifth Party Congress (1907) 64, 66, 68
    intervention after Revolution *14*
    and revolution in Britain 105
    and Russian Civil War 103

Second Party Congress (1903) 12, 58
    and Spain 152
    World War II 176–8
Brotherhood Church 64
Broz, Josep (Tito) 199, *199*
Budapest, Hungary 22
Bukharin, Nikolai *146*, 147, 150
Bulganin, Nikolai 212, *213*, 214
Bullock, Alan 17
Butovo Estate, Moscow *7*, 8

Castro, Fidel *21*
Charkviani, Father Christopher 36, 39
Chavchavadze, Prince Ilia 46, 47, *47*, 49
Chechnya 47, 182, 184
Cheka 101, *101*, 143
Chernyshevsky, Nikolai *45*, 46
Chuikov, Vasily 180
Church *7*, 197
Church School, Gori 39–41
Churchill, Winston *177*, 177–8, *181*, 182, 189–90, *190*, 191–4
    iron curtain speech 192, *192*
Civil War 102–4, 106
Cold War 192
collectivization 122, 125, 132–5, 137
convict labour *126*–7, *127*–9
Cossacks 195
Crimea *164*–5, 184, 190
Cult of Personality 117, 143, 150, 161, 196, 216
culture 140–1, 207–9

Davitashvili, Mikhail 51–2
Davrichewy, Joseph 36, 40
Davrichewy, David 37
de-Stalinization 216–18
dekulakization 132–6
Djugashvili, Besarion ('Beso') 32–6, 33, 38,–40, 42–3
Djugashvili, Ekaterina (née Geladze) ('Keke') *32*, 32–6, 38–40, 42–3, 49
Djugashvili, Vasily(Stalin's son) 201, *202*
Djugashvili, Yakov (Stalin's son) 63, 72, 168
Djugashvili, Zaza 35
'Doctors Plot' 211–12
Dzerzhinsky, Felix *101*, 143

East Germany 197–8, *203*
economy
    Five Year Plans 121, 122–37, 139, 141

New Economic Policy (NEP) 111–12
Egnatashvili, Yakov 36, 40
Enukidze, Avel 60
Eremin Letter (1937) 75
Eristavi, Elizabar 35, *35*
Etinger, Yakov 211–12
exile 56–7, 74, 77, *78*–9, 80–4, *81*–3, 90–2

famine 16, 134, 136, 195–6
farming
    collectivization 122, *125*, 132–6, 137
February Revolution (1917) 91–2, 92
Fifth Congress of the Russian Social Democratic Workers' Party (1907) 64, 66, 68
Five Year Plans 121, 122–37, 139, 141
    agriculture 122, *125*, 132–6, 137
    hero projects 130–1
    industry *122*–3, 124–8, 130–1
France 103, 152
Franco, Francisco 152
Freud, Sigmund 84

Gapon, Father Gregory *58*, 59
Geneva Convention (1929) 170
Georgia
    autonomy of 112–13
    de-Stalinization 218
    invasion of 113–14
    peasant uprising 35
    Russo-Georgian war (2008) 30
    see also Gori, Georgia; Tbilisi (Tiflis)
Germany
    post-war 197–8
    and revolution 105
    and Spain 152
    see also World War I; World War II
Gesse, Natalya 187
Glorification of Stalin (painting) *205*
Gori, Georgia 39
    childhood home of Stalin 31, *31*, *34*, *35*, 42
    Church School 39–41
    Stalin Museum 25, *26*–7, 28, 29–30, *30*, *200*
Gorky, Maxim 64
GPU (State Political Directorate) 143
Grand Alliance 177–8, 189–90
Great Purge 144–51
    death toll 16
    show trials 148–50
    types of people executed *7*–9
Gromyko, Andrei 206

221